Led By Donkeys

Led By Donkeys

How four friends with a ladder took on Brexit

Atlantic Books

London

Published in hardback in Great Britain in 2019 by Atlantic Books, an imprint of Atlantic Books Ltd.

Illustrations on pages 116-119 by Carl Glover.

10 9 8 7 6 5 4

A CIP catalogue record for this book is available from the British Library.

Hardback ISBN: 978 1 83895 019 4
E-book ISBN: 978 1 83895 020 0

Printed in Malta by Gutenberg Press Ltd

The papers used in the production of this title are Woodfree environmentally friendly papers with all sources used in their production from European Farmed Forests.

This paper is also ISO 9706, therefore it is paper made to Archival status with a long life of over 200 years minimum, conforming to EU and USA standards.

The cover material and the boards are both FSC certified.

Atlantic Books
An imprint of Atlantic Books Ltd
Ormond House 26-27 Boswell Street London WC1N 3JZ

www.atlantic-books.co.uk

For Lorna, Tabs, Emily and Kajsa

Our thanks to Leyla, without whom much of this would never have happened.

Like most good ideas, it was born down the pub.

We're four friends who manage to meet up only rarely, but one evening in December 2018 we're seated at a window table in The Birdcage in Stoke Newington, passing a phone around and shaking our heads with incredulity. On the screen is a tweet by David Cameron, posted three years earlier in the days before the 2015 general election:

> ● Britain faces a simple and inescapable choice – stability and strong Government with me, or chaos with Ed Miliband.

Theresa May has just cancelled the first meaningful vote on her Brexit deal and the state of the nation would not best be described as stable. Indeed, chaos has swept Westminster, and Cameron's plea has now been retweeted 18,000 times. It's the perfect encapsulation of Brexit – the imbecility and chronic underperformance of our political class; the arrogance; the lofty superiority juxtaposed against the shitstorm Cameron unleashed upon the country before retiring to a shepherd's hut.

'But he hasn't deleted it,' says Olly. 'You have to respect him for that.'

'Do you?' says Ben. 'Do you really?'

'Yeah. He's got rinsed for it every day for three years and he's not taken it down.'

'Suppose so.'

'It's a perfect tweet,' says Will. 'I hope it lives for ever.'

'It's truly a thing of beauty,' says James, staring down at the screen. 'Someone should print it out and put it in a museum.'

'Save it for future generations,' says Ben.

'So historians will know how arrogant and stupid our leaders were,' says Olly.

'A tweet you can't delete,' says Will.

And over the course of the next four or five minutes, almost fully formed, an idea emerges, one that within weeks will become the biggest entirely crowdfunded political campaign in British history. One of us suggests that we print out stickers of the tweet and slap them on windows and walls. Someone else says we could turn it into a flag and fly it from the flagpole of Cameron's local Conservative Association. We could put it on a banner and hire a plane to fly it through the sky above London. Or we could print it out and paste it up on that billboard over there, the one across the road on the A10. After all, a tweet is the shape of a billboard – it would fit perfectly. And why stop at Cameron? We could dig out the most offensive lies, lunacy and hypocrisy of our Brexit overlords and paste those up as well.

Tweets you can't delete.

Excitedly the four of us discuss locations and argue over who we might target. Olly is possessed of a visceral dislike for Michael Gove, while James has his sights on Liam Fox. Ben is uncompromising in his disdain for Dominic Raab, while Will wonders if it isn't possible to do them all, but if he has to choose – if he absolutely has to choose one of them – well, it would of course be Jacob Rees-Mogg.

And then, as is often the way with these things, the conversation veers onto something else, and something else after that, and by the time we pull on our coats and step out into the night the idea has all but evaporated. I mean, it's not actually going to happen, is it? We're four middle-aged fathers of young children, it's two weeks before Christmas and those presents aren't going to buy and wrap themselves. There are barely enough hours in

the day to get the kids fed and into bed, without taking on the delivery of an anti-Brexit guerrilla poster campaign.

We say our goodbyes without even mentioning it.

But the following day James pops up in our WhatsApp group.

> **James**: Hey guys, that poster idea. I've found a few places that actually print billboards and deliver them to you. Maybe we should do it. Thoughts?

Maybe we should. Nobody else is doing much to challenge the charlatans and knaves who dissembled and misled their way to a narrow referendum victory. Barely an hour passes without one of them appearing on the radio or television, propagandizing for the glories of a hard Brexit, as if their past record of contradictory predictions and pronouncements was non-existent. So yeah, we think, let's put up a few of those historic quotes on posters, but only after we've got the kids to sleep. It would be cathartic. And

hell, it would be a better use of our time than sitting on the sofa shouting febrile abuse at the news.

We don't plan to pay for the billboard sites; instead we'll temporarily borrow advertising real estate from companies that can afford to lend it to us. We just won't ask them first. Obviously one description of this arrangement would be 'criminal damage', so very deliberately we choose a large printing outfit located far from London, in the hope that the company won't even register what we've ordered, and if they do, they'll never see how we've deployed their product and report us to the police.

But who should feature in our campaign? Cameron, of course, but who else, and which of their tweets? In fact, do they even need to be tweets? Can't we simply dig out the wild predictions of the leading Brexiters, render them as tweets and paste them up? It would be visually arresting, far more so than simply putting up a quote in speech marks. A tweet is declarative, uncompromising, eye-catching. And it's the shape of a billboard.

We pepper the WhatsApp group with the most absurd claims made by the leading lights of Brexit – the ones we can remember, at least – and arrive at four examples of quite stunning sophistry:

The day after we vote to leave we hold all the cards and can choose the path we want – Michael Gove

The Free Trade Agreement that we will do with the European Union should be one of the easiest in human history – Liam Fox

There will be no downside to Brexit, only a considerable upside – David Davis

Getting out of the EU can be quick and easy – the UK holds most of the cards in any negotiation – John Redwood

Will is a professional photographer with an eye for visual design. He opens Photoshop and creates the first posters, then pings the group.

> **Will**: Hey guys, quick question. Don't we need a name on these? What are we called?

What are we called? Do we even need a name? Well, at the very least we should tweet out pictures of our posters, so we'll need a Twitter handle. So, by extension, we need a name.

> **James**: Idea... a play on Lions Led By Donkeys. We can use it for general criticism of the arseholes in power

'Lions led by donkeys'. It was the phrase coined by German commanders in the First World War to describe the British infantry and their incompetent generals. Could it not accurately describe the British people and their Brexit leaders?

Olly: My only concern with Lions Led By Donkeys is that it shows your hand immediately. Do we see value in a strong but ambiguous name that takes people to a website packed with all their quotes?

Ben: Any ideas of alternatives? I tend to think LLBD kinda does what it says on the tin and there's a lot of value to that. We should decide by tomorrow lunchtime so I can get the posters ordered to arrive next week.

Olly: Okay I'm in for LLBD. It works. The people leading us into this moment are so incompetent and it's the raging incompetence that has to be at the centre of this

Ben: @Will, any chance of pdfs today? Or is kiddie craziness descending?

Will: Is this okay? But with #LedByDonkeys (without Lions)?

James: Yeah just #LedByDonkeys I reckon. Great work Will!

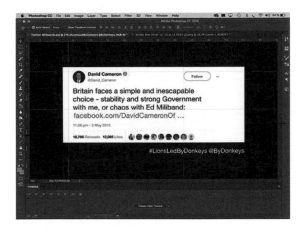

Olly: Yup, great

Ben:

It's surprisingly cheap to buy a billboard. Not the actual advertising space (we're stealing that), but the paper sheets that are pasted up. We assume that ordering five 6 x 3m posters will set us back the best part of £1,000, but in reality each poster is forty quid and delivery is free. Ben orders the posters, and two days later a huge cardboard envelope the size of the man delivering it is deposited on his doorstep.

Ben waits until after he's put his one-year-old daughter to bed before cutting open the cardboard. On the front of the envelope is a false name. No sense making it any easier for an officious Brexiter at the printer's to report us, he thinks. But then these guys probably ship out dozens, hundreds, *thousands* of these posters every day. They likely won't give our project a second look. Right?

Wrong. There are five envelopes within the cardboard. Ben slides out the top one and opens it. It's Cameron. Inside are twelve sheets, each one measuring 1 x 1.5m. And stuck to the underside of the envelope is an A4 rendition of the design, with faint lines on it that show how all the pieces fit together. Ben glances at the miniature version of what we will soon be plastering on a giant billboard.

'Oh, wow!' he mutters.

Protruding from David Cameron's head are two devil horns.

For a moment Ben wonders if this is Will's idea of a joke, but on closer inspection he sees that the horns have been drawn on with a biro. Is our printer an avid Brexiter who despises Cameron for his role in the Remain campaign or a pro-EU activist whose fury has been aroused by the former PM's botched handling of the referendum?

The giant envelope sits in the corner of Ben's living room next to a nappy-changing mat, and over the following

days it becomes obscured by a growing pile of Christmas presents. But it can't be ignored. It stinks (the envelope, not the nappy mat). The sheets are made of a blue-backed paper that emits a powerful chemical whiff and Ben worries it might be poisoning his daughter, so he locks the envelope in his car. At the same time Parliament goes into recess and the Brexit war goes into abeyance. Out of sight, out of mind. Led By Donkeys has stalled on the starting line.

But then Christmas and New Year pass and the news roars back. Mayhem envelops Westminster like a hurricane making landfall. The faces of Rees-Mogg, Redwood and Johnson return to our screens, all complaining that May's deal with the EU represents servitude and vassalage, despite all of them having claimed in 2016 that the EU would crumble before the awesome might of Britain's negotiating position.

It's too much to bear. We jump onto a Skype call. We have to do this, we agree. We have to get those damn posters up. We debate which one to launch with and whether Cameron (a Remainer) should even be in the mix. As it is, we agree to start with the former prime minister, but to use him as a practice run. It was, after all, his white-hot political ineptitude that got us into this mess.

'We'll just do the Cameron one and see how it goes,' says Olly.

'Put it up, see if people get it,' says Will.

'Proof of concept,' says James.

'Okay, good,' says Ben. 'Let's do it.' Silence. 'Just one thing. How do you actually put up a billboard?'

There is a critical dearth of online information for the amateur poster-paster to access. No tutorials, no easy-to-follow guides. It's not like tips on baking a lemon-drizzle cake or fixing a puncture. You're on your own.

How hard can it be? we wonder. *Possibly very hard indeed*, we conclude. Eventually we find a YouTube video shot by a painter and decorator who's made a time-lapse of himself pasting up an advert for his own business, on a 6 x 3m site. We scrutinize his video, the way a detective might

study CCTV footage of a crime scene. Every detail is pored over for clues. For a day the WhatsApp group becomes a specialist discussion forum. *How thick is his paste? What kind of roller is he using? How large is the overlap between the sheets? In what order does he paste them?* So exhaustive is our study of the discipline, so obsessed have we become with the science of putting up a billboard, that we rename the WhatsApp group *#PosterChat* – a name that sticks for the rest of the project.

From B&Q Ben orders a £90 ladder, two buckets, two paint rollers and a generous supply of wallpaper paste. Because his partner is six months pregnant, with their baby due, of all days, on 29 March (Brexit Day), he has the kit delivered to his work. For several days it sits behind his desk, eliciting puzzled looks and occasional comments from colleagues about home improvement.

That weekend he rides his bike up the A10, past the site we identified three weeks earlier from that pub window. It's on a slope, not steep, but uneven enough to make him wonder whether the ladder will be stable. He pedals around the corner onto Manor Road to look at another billboard. Below this one the pavement is flat. The bottom of the billboard is at head height, but the ladder would just about reach the top, he thinks. And it's covered in an advert for a bank.

It's perfect.

8–13 January 2019 ✓
@ByDonkeys

We're Ben Stewart, James Sadri, Olly Knowles and Will Rose — four friends in our late thirties and forties with backgrounds in environmental and human-rights activism.

Will is a freelance photographer with a long and storied record of climbing power-station smokestacks across Europe to document climate-change protests. He's originally from just outside Newcastle, but met a Swedish woman seven years ago and moved to a town north of Gothenburg where they're raising two kids. For him, Brexit is personal.

Olly writes strategies for the Greenpeace global-oceans campaign, working with teams around the world to bring projects to life. He's been picketing, shutting down and locking onto the objects of his political ire since he was a teenager. His grandfather lost his parents and sister in a V-1 rocket strike in the Second World War — to see the hard-won prize of a unified and peaceful Europe put at risk for vacuous notions of 'Global Britain' is, for Olly, quite baffling.

James works as a consultant advising organizations on digital campaigning, but his passion is getting people to close their laptops and do something in the real world. His father is British and his mother Iranian and he grew up aware of the stark contrast between the rights and freedoms afforded to the two sides of his family, knowing that some of them could roam the world as they pleased with their British passports, while others had to pay people smugglers to flee conflict. So he always regarded the EU as

an imperfect but inspiring way of organizing neighbouring societies – not as a collection of competing nation states but as something that saw its citizens as people first and nationalities later.

Ben cut his teeth as a press officer at Greenpeace and now oversees the various media functions at the organization, specializing in writing and strategic communications (telling stories that make change happen). He grew up in Folkestone, where on a clear day he could see France from his school. The fields he ran through as a kid were later requisitioned to build the Channel Tunnel terminal. He feels European. Always has.

Over the years each of us has gradually accrued more responsibility in our personal and professional lives – children to raise, colleagues to manage and budgets to balance. But the EU referendum and the rise of right-wing populism has sparked in us a renewed desire to get stuck in.

Brexit was a heist. That's what we think. The last two years have felt like standing outside a branch of Barclays watching a band of bank robbers stroll out with their ill-gotten loot slung over their shoulders, before clambering into a getaway car and roaring away unchallenged, as the cops stand on the pavement swinging their truncheons and shrugging their shoulders. When Michael Gove appears on the news to justify the compromises Theresa May is making in the face of a united European Union negotiating position, one of us might shout at the interviewer, 'Just ask him if we still hold all the fucking cards!' And when Jacob Rees-Mogg or Nigel Farage warns that a People's Vote would represent an unconscionable affront to democracy, we wonder when someone – anyone – is going to throw back at them their historic support for a second referendum. We wonder why disgraced former Defence Secretary Liam Fox is allowed to get through the first thirty seconds of any interview without being asked to account for his claim that a trade deal with the EU should be the easiest in human history. And we're utterly perplexed that hard Brexiter Owen Paterson is never challenged on

his previous assertion that 'only a madman' would leave the Single Market. And then there are the sundry atrocities and hypocrisies of Boris Johnson.

Yes, Brexit was a heist, and the people who were meant to catch the getaway car – the interviewers and opposition politicians whose privilege it is to hold our leaders to account – are displaying scant interest in their historic claims. So now, two years too late, we're going to chase down the Brexiters with a ninety-quid ladder from B&Q and a bucket of paste.

Olly and Ben live in London, James is in Bristol and Will is back in Sweden, so rather than assembling as a foursome to attempt the Cameron poster, we decide that Ben and Olly will attempt to put it up. It is, after all, just a practice run. If it proves as difficult as we fear, we have another four designs with which to perfect our technique.

On the second Tuesday of January Olly puts his kids to bed, then drives two miles across London to Ben's house. As he clambers into the car, Olly looks at him quizzically.

'Where's the ladder?'

'At work.'

'At *work*?'

'Behind my desk at work. All the stuff's still there. Can we swing by the office first?'

Twenty minutes later we're standing in front of a sink outside the toilets at Greenpeace, mixing wallpaper paste. As we leave the office carrying a ladder and a bucket of watery paste, the security guard behind the reception desk looks up from his computer.

'Decorating the nursery,' says Ben over his shoulder as we push open the door.

On the drive back to Stoke Newington we rehearse the details of our strategy for posting the billboard. We've numbered the sheets one to twelve: the first six will go along the top, with seven to twelve along the bottom.

'So we're going one, seven; two, eight; three, nine, et cetera,' says Olly.

'Yup. And a 2cm crossover on each sheet. Also, you

should know it's pretty high up. The bottom of the board is at head height.'

'I'm not good with heights. Do you wanna go up?'

'The thing is,' says Ben, 'I think I might have labyrinthitis.'

'Sorry – what?'

'Labyrinthitis. I started feeling dizzy yesterday. It's like being seasick all the time. I'm not sure I should be climbing the ladder.'

'Huh. Very convenient timing.'

'Sorry, mate.'

'Laber-what?'

'Labyrinthitis.'

'So I'm going up the ladder, am I?'

'Is that okay?'

Olly sniffs.

'It'll have to be, won't it?'

We park the car on a quiet side street, unhitch the ladder from the roofrack and pull on luminous yellow high-visibility vests. We discussed on *#PosterChat* (the WhatsApp group) what we should wear for the operation – stay incognito by donning all black, wear our normal clothes or dress like professionals? It was Olly who persuaded us to go with the pro look. 'Need to own the space,' he said. 'Trust me, if you look like you belong, then nobody questions you.'

We carry the ladder, buckets, rollers and twelve sheets across the road and look up at the billboard. Above us, reaching nearly five metres above the pavement, is an advert for the Halifax bank. It's cold. Our breath is visible in the freezing air. We lean the ladder against the top of the billboard on the left side and slowly, cautiously, Olly puts his foot on the first step.

Halfway up he looks down and grimaces. 'It's bloody high up.'

We're both nervous. This is criminal damage; it's the A10, police cars pass here all the time. We don't want to get arrested, we both have to take the kids to school and nursery in the morning. Ben dips a roller into the bucket, climbs a few steps and hands it to Olly, who runs it over

the top left of the Halifax ad. Then Ben hands him a tightly rolled tube. Sheet one of the Cameron poster. Olly holds it square with one hand at the top of the billboard, then unrolls it, smoothing it down with paste. But as he unrolls the bottom of the sheet, the top curls away from the board. He reaches up to re-stick it, but then the bottom slips down and he loses control of the paper. The picture of Cameron's face is sliding over the billboard like an ice cube on a tabletop. 'Argh!' Olly groans and passes the roller down to Ben. 'Quick, more paste.'

Ben dips the roller into the bucket and passes it up, watery gloop splatting onto his forehead. Olly rolls it over the sheet but he's losing control of the paper. The sheet peels away entirely and wraps itself around his head – David Cameron's face now plastered to Olly's as he teeters five metres up a ladder on the busy junction of Manor Road and the A10. As Olly wrestles with the sheet, the traffic light turns red and cars begin to back up directly below him. Ben can see drivers craning their necks to better observe the spectacle.

The dream is over. The project is dead before it even had a chance to live.

But eventually Olly frees himself from Cameron's embrace and, with a heave, slaps the sheet back against the billboard.

'The paste is way too thin,' he calls down. 'Do we have another sachet?'

'Stay there,' Ben shouts up, and as Olly throws his body against the sheet to keep it stuck to the board, Ben runs back to the car. A minute later he's pouring powder into the bucket.

'Here, try this.'

Olly reaches down, his stubble now thick with paste, takes the roller, then slaps it against the paper and with his other hand he pushes the sheet into the top-left corner. Furiously he runs the roller over the paper. It just about holds. He comes down a few rungs, Ben passes him the next sheet, he aligns it with the other one as best he can, then pastes it up. He descends to the pavement and we

look at each other. Both of our faces are dripping with wallpaper paste. It's in our eyes and mouths. When we speak it sprays from our lips.

'This is really bloody hard,' says Olly.

'Do you wanna call it a night?'

'No, we can do this. It's just going to take ages.'

'It's looking good, though. I mean, you did well. It's going to look great.'

We move the ladder over and Olly climbs back up, clutching the roller and the next sheet. For several minutes he wrestles with the paper until he's managed to secure it so that the words just about match up with sheet one. The paste is freezing and makes our hands ache with cold, so it's increasingly hard to place the sheets precisely. There is much desperate pushing and sliding and adjusting to get the words to align – a giant 18 sq/m vertical moving jigsaw. Drivers are looking up with perplexed expressions. This is very obviously not a professional operation, or if it is, then it's going badly wrong.

But slowly, from left to right, the tweet emerges. By the time we're pasting the eighth and ninth sheets it's clear to drivers that this is actually activism, because some start tooting their horns and unwinding their windows to give us the thumbs up. A cyclist pulls up next to Ben, gazes at the billboard, then looks him straight in the eye and says with some intensity, 'Nice, man. *Nice.*'

One hour and forty minutes after starting, the corners of sheet twelve are pasted down. Olly descends to the pavement, we pull off our high-vis vests and wipe our hands on each other's coats, then we cross the road and look up at the poster. Seeing it for the first time – a tweet blown up that big and turned into a billboard – we both instinctively know there's something about it that really works.

Olly drapes an arm around Ben's shoulder. 'That,' he says, 'is absolutely beautiful.'

We scoop up the bucket and roller and drag the ladder back to the car, fix it to the roof and climb in. Olly turns the ignition, then Ben says, 'Fancy a pint?'

'Christ, yes.'

'Birdcage?'

'Seems appropriate.'

As we walk around the corner onto the A10, passing under the billboard, Ben says, 'I think this might be quite a big deal. I mean, it does something to you, seeing it there, doesn't it?'

'It really does.'

'But we need to be mentally prepared to get seven retweets off this.'

'Expectation management?'

'A little bit, yeah.'

As we sip our pints a few minutes later, Olly checks his phone. He's on a WhatsApp group with a bunch of Hackney mates and one of them has posted a photo of him up the ladder with Ben standing underneath, clearly taken as they drove past us. *Guerilla tactics on Stamford Hill!* says the message. Two replies follow: *Ha! Love it!* and *Social Media at its best!*

'They don't know it's me,' says Olly.

'We've already gone viral,' says Ben.

The next day Ben takes a detour on his way back from nursery to take a picture of the billboard. He's half-convinced it won't still be there, but as he walks up the A10 he's thrilled to see it looming over the traffic. The tweet looks even better in the daylight. He snaps a few photos and retreats to a café, opens up his laptop and taps out the first tweet from the @ByDonkeys account.

> ⬤ Last night we started a little project to record for posterity the prophetic words of our leaders. Here's the first one (Manor Rd / A10 in London). Eyes peeled for more #LedByDonkeys #TweetsYouCantDelete

He attaches the photo, his finger hovers over the *send* button, then he pushes down. We're live. The project has

launched. He pings the WhatsApp group to tell the others. All four of us stare at our screens, waiting for the tweet to catch fire.

And precisely nothing happens.

It's hard to imagine why we thought it would be any other way, given that we don't have a single follower, but nevertheless the lack of traction is a disappointment. If a tree falls in a forest and nobody sees it, have you wasted an evening getting soaked in freezing wallpaper paste? Eventually we take to *#PosterChat*, to discuss who we could ask to give us a retweet and get the ball rolling. Ben messages *Guardian* columnist Marina Hyde, who follows him on his personal account, and asks if she might give it a kick.

Ben I am dead, she replies. *I love this.*

A minute later she's retweeted us and the whole thing explodes.

Olly: Light fuse.... retire

Ben: We're away. We have nearly 100 followers already

James: Amazing, it's taking off

Will: We're getting a lot of love in the notifications

Ben: 200 followers already

Olly: Oh boy!

James: Perfect start

Ben: 314 followers

Ben: First interview request in. TalkRadio. What do we think???

James: Do it man. Unless you think worth holding off for something?

Ben: I might just do it, even if it's with Julia Hartley-Brewer or something. Only concern is that I'm off sick today with labyrinthitis so don't really want it to be heard by colleagues.

Will: Ha!

James: Amazing momentum guys – what do you think about putting another one up asap to build on it? I'm free to come to London this evening if you're up for it??

Ben: Let's do it. If we put up Davis tonight that would be a helluva thing

Olly: Yeah let's do it

James: We've got to harness the momentum, this is going to be massive. I'm getting on the train after work. We're going straight out and doing another one!

Ben: Gary Kemp from Spandau Ballet is following us

By now scores of people are throwing Brexiter quotes at us and demanding that we get them up in their towns and cities. We're being presented with examples of such tremendous hypocrisy that none of us has seen before, and *#LedByDonkeys* is trending on Twitter. Olly, Ben and James seek permission from their partners to go out again, while

Will sets about finding a location. He uses a website that plots all the billboard sites in Britain, then cross-references with Google Street View to find an accessible site on a busy road – not so high this time and near where Olly and Ben live. We jump onto a Skype call to finalize the plan.

'Is Clapton okay?' asks Will.

'Clapton's great,' says Ben. 'It's near my house and my kid's not sleeping right now and Lorna is so pregnant, so I'll have to rush back if she needs me at home.'

'It's quite low down,' says Will. 'You won't be so high up tonight, Olly.'

'I'm going up again, am I?'

'I still have labyrinthitis,' says Ben.

'What's that?' asks James.

'Fear of heights,' says Olly.

On his way home Ben swings by the Cameron poster to marvel at our work. But the tweet is now covered in sky-blue sheets. Primesight – the owners of the billboard – have already removed our poster. By now the picture has been seen by hundreds of thousands of people online, we have 3,000 followers and Led By Donkeys has launched successfully, but seeing last night's work covered up is still a bitter disappointment.

That night Olly picks the others up in his car – ladder on the roof, pre-mixed paste in the boot – and we set out to deploy David Davis. We park the car down a quiet road, wary as we are of number-plate recognition cameras, then carry the kit to the site Will has identified. But when we get there we're confronted with a mighty pink billboard emblazoned with a picture of a suffragette and the slogan *FEMINISTS DON'T WEAR PINK*. We're not sure if a crew of guerrilla poster-pasters has got there before us, if a feminist campaign group has paid for the image to go up, or (most likely) if it's a corporate message attempting to sell stuff by co-opting a social movement.

'I don't think we can paste over this,' says Ben. 'It might be part of some brilliant campaign, and then we'd look like dickheads.'

The next billboard along the road is covered in peeling paper and a barely recognizable image of the Empire State Building.

'Let's do that one instead,' says Olly.

And we get to work.

There is a concept in Japanese business known as *Kaizen*. It roughly translates as *continuous progress* and refers to a rapid-improvement event in which a small team devotes all its energies over a short period of time to analysing and solving a narrowly defined process issue. We've spent a good portion of the past twelve hours on *#PosterChat* discussing the pasting technique we adopted the previous night for Cameron – its merits and its limitations and what we might do to improve it. Crucially, we agreed that 7 litres of water per sachet resulted in near-disaster. So among a series of refinements we've dropped that down to 4.

Within the first two sheets of the Davis poster we know we've made huge strides. The paper is sticking effortlessly to the backboard, and by the time we've got six sheets up we're buzzing at our own efficiency.

'Only twenty minutes gone,' says Olly.

'Halfway already,' says James.

'What is it about David Davis that makes him such a prick?' says Ben, running a roller over the poster. 'He's arrogant, I get that. But it's something else.'

'I think it's the combination of arrogance and nuclear stupidity,' says Olly, handing down his own roller for a paste refreshment. 'Did you see that thing he said during the campaign about German CEOs knocking down Merkel's door after Brexit, demanding that she give Britain a trade deal?'

'I think that's it,' says Ben. 'It's the way he says stupid stuff like it's the most obvious, blinding truth.'

Suddenly a police car screams over the top of the hill to our left, siren blaring. It speeds down the road, then skids to a stop next to us. And it just sits there. The doors don't open. The officers inside stare straight ahead. Olly looks down from the top of the ladder and hisses, 'Own the

space.' James nonchalantly stirs the bucket of paste, Ben taps a rolled-up sheet in the palm of his hand, as in his head he goes through the plan we agreed on if we're quizzed by the police (claim to be professional billboard operatives, give the cops the number of an advertising company and urge them to call it, hoping nobody will answer at 9 p.m.).

But then, just as abruptly as it arrived, the police car pulls away and speeds off.

We all exhale, shake our heads with relief and get back to work. Soon we've finished pasting up the last sheets. We cross the road and stare at the billboard.

> ● @DavidDavisMP – There will be no downside to Brexit, only a considerable upside

'He really is an arsehole,' says Ben.

'Poster looks good, though,' says Olly.

The whole operation has taken less than three-quarters of an hour to complete. Rapid improvement indeed.

* * *

The next morning we tweet out a picture. Amid general excitement about the project and an ever-growing Twitter follower-count, there is a common refrain – that we're simply 'Remoaners' preaching to the tribe within the M25 bubble. It's a fair point, we think. Our first two posters have been pasted in Hackney North and Stoke Newington – the third most anti-Brexit constituency in the UK. If one of the things we're trying to achieve is to start a conversation amongst Leave voters about the promises we were all made by leading Brexiters, it's unlikely we'll spark it by putting up billboards opposite the organic markets and vegan bicycle-repair cafés of east London.

So, next stop: Romford.

The town voted 70 per cent Leave and has become synonymous with an outer-London rejection of the city's progressive, cosmopolitan core. But the reason we choose it for our third hit is practical – it's the only Leave-voting town we can get to and back, including pasting, in under three hours.

As it is, only Olly can make it, so he recruits a friend from work who grew up in Romford and knows its streets well. Three nights after doing David Davis, they unpack the Gove poster from the envelope and pull out the A4 version supplied by the printers. While the Cameron sheet was decorated with devil horns, Michael Gove's forehead has been scrawled over in biro with a single word: CUNT.

Our printers are not the bureaucratic Brexiters of our imagination.

It takes just over an hour to get the poster up (not bad, given that half the team has never done this before), and as the two of them stand back and look up, they nod with satisfaction.

> ⬤ @MichaelGove – The day after we vote to leave, we hold all the cards and we can choose the path we want

15 January 2019 ✅

@ByDonkeys

There's something about Dominic Raab that is volcanically dislikeable. Ambition and arrogance combined with incompetence and pulsating cynicism, he's one of those Leave MPs about whom you wonder if they even believe in Brexit or if their position is instead a product of a craven determination to become prime minister.

By now we've ordered a second batch of posters, and Raab is one of the ones we've had printed up: '*I hadn't quite understood the full extent of this but... we are particularly reliant on the Dover–Calais crossing.*' An extraordinary thing for the then-Brexit secretary to have said. Of course the government is packed with various shades of Raab – they're all putting career before country – but this quote is not even from a Freedom of Information request. It wasn't leaked. He said it at a conference. He's so ignorant that he didn't even know he was being ignorant.

But where should we paste it? There's really only one town to take it to – the frontline of Brexit. Dover is a two-hour drive from London and this will be our fourth guerrilla operation in eight nights.

Olly pulls up outside Ben's house and hoots his horn. It's Tuesday 15 January, the night of the first meaningful vote on Theresa May's Brexit deal. Ben and James come out onto the street, dragging four black bin liners, each containing twelve rolled-up posters. By now we've honed our technique and feel confident taking on more than one site in a night. We load the bags into the boot beside two buckets brimming with thick paste. James is carrying a broom.

'What's that for?' asks Olly.

'I know you guys are all about the rollers, but I've been speaking to a decorator and he reckons the professional wallpaper guys use a soft-brush broom,' says James.

'Interesting,' says Olly, nodding slowly and biting his lip.

'You don't sound convinced.'

'No, no, let's see – let's see.'

As we pull away, Olly turns on BBC Radio 5 live. 'What, do you feel the rollers aren't working?' he asks.

'It's not that,' says James, cradling his new broom in the back seat. 'I just think we should be prepared to innovate.'

'Okay,' says Olly quietly, staring at the road ahead.

The radio presenter cuts to the Commons for the result. Most pundits are predicting a defeat for the government, with some warning that May might go down by as many as 150 votes.

'The ayes to the right: two hundred and two; the noes to the left: four hundred and thirty-two.'

Two hundred and thirty. It's a catastrophic defeat for the prime minister and her Brexit plan. As we head south we plan our night.

'Can we put Raab up first?' asks Ben. 'Honestly, I'd like to get them all up, but that sociopath is going up in Dover. I don't care if we get nicked, as long as we do Raab.'

'Agreed,' says Olly. 'Raab is the priority. Then Fox?'

'Raab, then Fox, then Mogg, then May, I reckon,' says James. 'But Raab first. Absolutely.'

'What if May resigns tomorrow?' says Ben. 'Would a May poster be redundant then?'

'It would be a good problem to have,' says Olly.

From Sweden, Will has identified four sites for us in Dover, which we've marked up on a printed map with thumbnail photos from Street View so we can see what we'll be faced with. One of the sites is low, maybe just a foot off the pavement, and the easiest to tackle. Given that we've just committed above all else to get Raab up, we decide to do him there.

'It shouldn't be too high for you, Olly,' says Ben, studying the photo in the passenger seat.

Olly turns his head. 'Still got your labyrinth disease?'

'Can't seem to shake it.'

James holds a flask out between the front seats. 'Coffee, anyone?'

'Is it instant or filter?' says Ben.

'Instant. Why?'

'I'm allergic to instant coffee.'

'You're allergic to instant coffee?'

'Yeah.'

'People like you. You're why Brexit happened.'

As soon as we pull into Dover we know this night will be different. It isn't Hackney, obviously, but this isn't even Romford. The main shopping street, London Road, is peppered with discount shops and boarded-up windows. The only places open are a couple of pubs, though they seem largely deserted. A homeless man shelters in a shop front. It's almost a cliché of the broken, left-behind community that nurtured the justifiable resentments that bred Brexit. Will we meet opposition in the street? Will the posters even work in this different context? Will the police take a much closer look at us? It's one thing putting these billboards up in Stoke Newington, where drivers wind down the window to give you a thumbs up. But now, here, tonight in Dover, we're nervous.

'It's always been like this,' says Ben, who grew up just a few miles away. 'This isn't new. Some parts of Folkestone have it even worse. People struggle round here, always have done. I'm almost surprised it took so long for the backlash.'

We pull up around the corner from our first site. We're in a tight cluster of small terraced fishermen's houses on narrow streets. A few lights are on, but most of the houses are dark. It's just after 10 p.m. and completely quiet. As we unstrap the ladder from the roofrack, the ping of metal sounds explosively loud. Without speaking we carry the kit

100 metres and rest it against the wall next to the billboard. It's covered with an advert for McDonald's. A few metres across the road is a window with open curtains, through which we can see a couple watching television. Silently we set to work.

Olly climbs the ladder with his roller and Ben mounts a milk crate (a new addition to our armoury). James holds up his brush for Olly to take. Olly eyes it suspiciously.

'Just try it,' James urges.

Olly sighs and exchanges the roller for the brush, steadies himself and sweeps the soft bristles over the top-left corner of the board. It delivers a thick and even layer of paste. James passes him the first sheet, which sticks immediately, then Olly sweeps over it with the brush. The creases smooth out easily, and soon enough Raab's face is visible in the perfect position.

'This brush isn't too bad,' Olly says absently.

James looks down at his shoes and nods.

A door opens a few houses down the road and a young guy comes out, crosses the street, slows down as he passes us, then looks up. He scrutinizes each of us in turn, reads the poster, sniffs and walks away. We each let out a deep breath.

Unlike on our previous operations, we feel genuinely exposed in Dover. What we're doing is obviously Remain activism. We're on the frontline of Brexit in a town that voted heavily for Leave and has sometimes been the venue for far-right protest marches. And here we are, ostentatiously pasting up illegal 18 sq/m anti-Brexit propaganda posters. We might as well be wearing blue T-shirts with yellow stars and singing the EU anthem 'Ode to Joy'. And yet the couple watching TV never look away from the screen.

It takes us thirty-five minutes to paste up the poster. We stand back and admire our work.

These things are subjective, of course, but we feel we're looking at a thing of exquisite beauty. We've got Raab up in Dover and it's quite exhilarating. As we pack up the ladder and carry the kit back to the car, each of us feels that even if

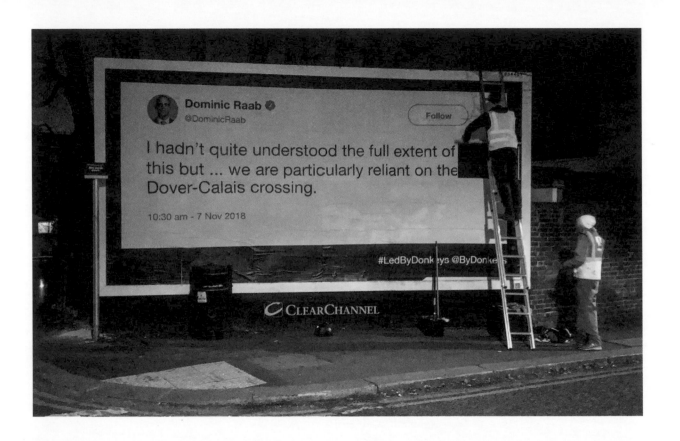

the project ends right here – even if a police officer is at this moment sitting in the driver's seat of Olly's car, filling out a charge sheet for criminal damage – it will have been worth it.

As it is, we're on the road again a few minutes later, Ben scrutinizing Will's map. 'This one is quite high up,' he says. Then, looking closer at the picture, he adds, 'Actually it looks *really* high.'

When we pull up under the site, Ben winds down the window and we all look up. Another McDonald's advert covers a billboard above a platform bolted high onto the side of a house overlooking the car park of an MOT centre. It would take most of the length of the ladder just to get us onto the platform, then we'd have to haul up the kit. By the time Olly got to the top of the ladder he'd be operating seven metres above the ground, and we'd all be working on a rickety metal platform that looks like it could easily cave away from the wall.

'Do we fancy this one?' asks Ben.

'It looks pretty dodgy,' says James. 'And look, there's a bedroom window right next to the billboard. It's on the side of someone's house. Maybe find another site?'

'Oh, come on,' says Olly. 'Let's do it. It's time for Liam Fox. Easiest trade deal in history. Epic donkey, epic quote. Needs an epic location. Come on!'

Silence.

'It *would* be immense,' says Ben.

'A lot of people would see it,' says James.

A few minutes later we're hauling the ladder up onto the platform, then balancing it against the top of the house. Below us, across the road, the Kong Sing Chinese takeaway is doing a steady trade. If we felt exposed putting up Raab, then this feels like a burglary. That bedroom window is covered by curtains, but we'll be operating just a metre of two away from it. We each hold a finger to our lips and nod. We'll have to do this one in complete silence.

The first few sheets go up easily enough. There's a queue in the takeaway but nobody is looking up, and even if they do, they won't be able to make out much in

the darkness. We use a form of improvised sign language to ask each other for more paste or for help positioning a sheet, or for a towel to wipe the freezing paste from our hands. Then, just as we're securing sheet ten on the bottom row, a piercing bark breaks the silence. *Yap! Yap! Yap!* A dog is growling and clawing at the wall below us, trying to reach our ankles, biting at the metal grate of the platform. We freeze and stare at each other.

'Own the space,' Olly whispers. 'Look like we belong.'

We turn back to the poster, but a moment later there's a whooshing sound, like a surge of energy passing through us, as from each corner of the car park a floodlight switches on and bathes us in brilliant white light. We lift our hands to shield our eyes. The dog is going berserk now. Two heads appear in the doorway of the takeaway and look up. Is a security guard about to emerge from the MOT centre? If we're busted, there's no escape. The guard would merely have to stand below the platform, call the police and wait patiently for them to arrive. The same could be said for any

Brexit ultras queuing at that moment for crispy aromatic duck with special fried rice. They'd look up and see a trio of Remain activists committing criminal damage. And we could hardly deny it. The evidence is behind us in the form of an 18 sq/m Liam Fox billboard. How long would it take for them to assemble a crew to wait for us on the pavement?

Yap! Yap! Yap!

'Own. The fucking. Space,' Olly hisses.

'Do we abort?' says James.

'Five minutes to finish this thing,' Ben whispers. 'We can do it.'

Olly is already fixing the eleventh sheet. James looks at the almost-completed billboard, by now beautifully floodlit against the Dover skyline. *Easiest trade deal in human history, eh?* he thinks. *How's that going, Doctor?* And with renewed determination he dips a roller into the paste and gets back to work, and a few minutes later the last sheet is up. James climbs down to the pavement to grab a photo,

then we lower the ladder to the ground, ferry the kit down to the pavement and casually walk off round the corner to where the car is parked, watched all the way by a cluster of customers in the takeaway. As we drive past them, we dip our heads to hide our faces.

The final sites we've identified are in the town centre. Two billboards next to each other. By now it's past midnight. We park up and James and Olly unload the kit, as Ben strolls over to check out the boards. He can see a small pile of flowers under one of them and a stone plaque of remembrance. A young girl died at this spot and the anniversary has recently passed. Ben goes back to the car.

'The one on the left is a memorial. We can't do a protest on it. Imagine if this gets on the news – it'd really upset the family.'

'Okay, just one here then,' says Olly.

Before long we're pasting Jacob Rees-Mogg's face over an advert for the TV series *Luther*. It's our third board of the night, the sixth in the project, and by now we're a well-functioning team – Olly up the ladder doing the top sheets with the soft wire brush, Ben on the milk crate doing the bottom row, James supplying paste and posters, stabilizing the ladder and watching out for cops. The first two sheets are up in record time, so Olly comes down, James moves the ladder over, Olly whistles as he goes back up and James stands on the bottom rung. Then, as Olly finishes off the third sheet and comes down, he cries out – a pained, guttural howl that echoes down the empty streets of Dover.

'Awww, dog turd!'

He's coming down the ladder gingerly, holding the sides with his hands. James turns a torch onto the scene. Every rung is smeared in thick black excrement. Olly's boots – the original source – are caked in it. He reaches the pavement, turns round and holds his hands out, palms up. They're covered in it too. He wipes them on the towel, using it to clean the rungs as Ben and James stand back with pained expressions. Olly wipes down the rungs up to head height, but when he stands on the ladder to reach the ones higher up, he realizes he's merely spreading the mess over the lower rungs, so he jumps off and spins round.

'God, it's everywhere.'

The towel is by now thick and heavy with dog shit.

'Own the space?' Ben suggests.

'Piss off,' says Olly. 'You're not the one covered in poo.'

'Just push on through, man.'

'Oh, you want *me* to push on through, do you?'

'I've got labyrinth—'

'I think there's another towel in the car,' says James.

A minute later James is wiping down the ladder, while Olly stomps up and down the pavement, trying to bash off the excrement from his boots. Then he takes the brush and climbs the ladder, but with each rung crusts of turd fall from his soles and drop with almost perfect precision into the bucket of wallpaper paste.

'Whoah, Olly — stop!' James cries. 'You're dropping shit into the bucket.'

'Aww, crap,' says Olly, looking down. 'Can you pick it out?'

'Pick it out? Seriously?'

'Can you try?'

James bends over the bucket and reaches down with thumb and forefinger, then stops, shaking his head. 'I'm gonna have to stir it in,' he says. 'Sorry, mate.'

Olly passes down the brush and James dips it into the bucket, stirs it around, then passes it back.

'I've temporarily stopped having fun,' says Olly from the top of the ladder, running the shitty paste over Rees-Mogg's name. And for the next half an hour we paste up an anti-Brexit poster with diluted dog turd.

When it's done, we stand back and look up. The work is a little shoddy – more creases than we would have liked, and a couple of the sheets aren't well aligned. It's radiating a pungent whiff of poo. But it's up.

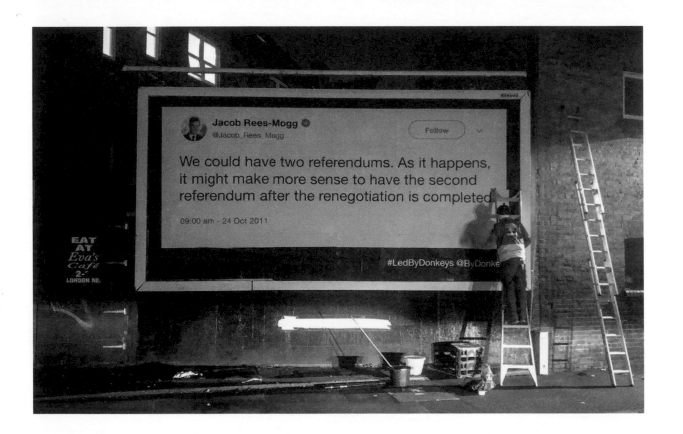

> @Jacob_Rees_Mogg – We could have two referendums. As it happens, it might make more sense to have the second referendum after the renegotiation is completed.

We're soon sat back in the car (windows open), discussing whether to do the fourth and final poster. It's now past 1 a.m.

'Let's just drive round and find a site,' says James. 'If you don't mind, Olly. I mean, obviously you're the one covered in dog shit.'

'Do I smell?' Olly asks.

'You can fit four pictures in a tweet, right?' says Ben.

'It's bad, isn't it?' says Olly.

'Yup, that's right, four pics in a tweet,' says James. 'We need one more.'

'Yeah, you stink,' says Ben.

We drive up London Road, looking for sites, and before long we spot a well-lit billboard on the side of a minicab office. We work quickly and just half an hour after starting, we have the prime minister up.

> @Theresa_May – Remaining a member of the European Union means we will be more secure from crime and terrorism.

Olly drives us down to a hotel on the seafront and James and Ben climb out. It's nearly 2 a.m. The plan is for two of us to stay over, then take the photos the next morning and tweet them out. James pulls out his phone and uploads four grainy iPhone pictures, one of each billboard, to *#PosterChat*. It's 3 a.m. in Sweden, but Will is checking the WhatsApp group.

Will: Holy. Fucking. SHIT!!!!!

Will: Massive massive respect!

Will: Looks amazing guys

Will: 👊 👊 👊

We say our goodbyes on the pavement, Ben and James gingerly hugging Olly as we offer each other congratulations for what we've just pulled off. Olly climbs back into his car and pulls away, heading for London.

The next morning Ben and James set out to get the pictures. It's thrilling to see the posters still up – we feared they'd have been vandalized or removed overnight. We have an hour before our train leaves, so we set up in the corner of a café. Various newspaper front pages are being held up around us, each telling the story of May's catastrophic defeat. We select the best photo from each of the sites and post them in one tweet:

> A busy night on the Brexit frontline. We've covered Dover in the historic quotes of the people responsible for this chaos. Britain is a nation #LedByDonkeys.

And this, more perhaps than any other moment, is when the project goes truly viral.

16–27 January 2019 ✓

@ByDonkeys

On the train back to London we watch as the retweets race into the thousands and our in-box fills with suggestions for new tweets and locations. It seems that on this morning, of all mornings, the Donkeys posters are satisfying people's need for an expression of the failure of the political class. Accidentally, haphazardly and with a dose of dog shit, our campaign has met the moment.

There is a lively discussion in the Twitter comments about whether or not the billboards have been Photoshopped, but then one Dover resident says he's popped down to the end of his road to check out Dominic Raab and can confirm the whole thing is real. We field calls from the Press Association, the BBC, the *Guardian* and a host of international newspapers. *#PosterChat* is alive with developments.

Ben: Guardian chat went well. One question was 'Are you members of the Labour Party or Momentum or Best for Britain? Will Corbyn be next?' I said we're focusing squarely on the people who run the country. He asked me if we have policies about what we cover up. I said we decided not to cover that feminist one with Davis but were happy to cover two McDonald's last night. Now I'm paranoid about a Rod Liddle hit piece about snooty Remainers who look down on people who eat at McD's

James: Firstly and lastly, fuck Rod Liddle

Olly: If we get that Rod Liddle piece the socialist champagne is on me

By now there are scores of demands that we set up a crowdfunder (an online push for funding from the public) and take the campaign national. And of course there's the usual trenchant, nit-picking dissatisfaction that accompanies anything even mildly popular on the Internet.

Ben: Seen this? One guy's saying 'I've a slight issue with these billboards. All posted in the southeast, it seems. When will we see one in the northeast?'

Will: Ha ha. That's brutal after a sleepless night in Dover

Ben: People will only be happy when we put one on the bloody moon

Our follower-count on Twitter is rising rapidly – so rapidly, in fact, that we decide to have some fun by chasing down and overtaking leading Brexiters. But who should be our first target? That much is obvious.

⬤ Let's expose the Brexit bullshit artists in front of as many people as possible. Can we get more followers than Prime Minister wannabe @DominicRaab? Raab: 30,928, ByDonkeys: 9,861. You know what to do. #DoverDenier

Any sense that Dover is the climax of the project, that our need for catharsis has been sated and we'll soon be winding down, is rendered redundant by the reaction. Many of the most influential journalists and commentators in the country are now following us, and we have a vaguely influential platform from which to offer our own commentary on the Brexit farce. We're being inundated

with suggestions for new posters – many of them examples of thermonuclear hypocrisy – and by the end of the day Will has knocked up five new designs and we're discussing where and when to strike next.

Ideally we'll hit the north-east, preferably Sunderland. Its place in the Brexit story was cemented when it declared early on the night of the EU referendum, and became the first indicator that Britain had voted to leave. Certainly we need to get out of the south-east – not to get that Twitter follower off our backs, but because he's right: Brexit is a national calamity, it was caused by (among other things) a geographical schism, and we don't want to play into that by being a radical band of Remoaner guerrillas pasting posters for the sole benefit of 'our people'. In fact, we all deplore the tribalism unleashed by Brexit.

But how can we get our posters up across the country, when we all have young kids? Until now we've been putting the children to bed, then pulling on our high-vis gear to paste up posters in the dark, but always (with the exception of Dover) getting back in time to get the kids to school and nursery in the morning. Sunderland is 300 miles away – it would be a long drive. Even if we got the billboard up in half an hour, the whole thing would be a twelve-hour operation. It just wouldn't be fair on our partners.

For the first time we start to entertain the possibility of setting up a crowdfunder. A lot of people are asking us to do it: they want to see the posters proliferate, they want to be involved, and donating cash would give them a way. It seems it isn't just us who find Led By Donkeys cathartic.

We chew it over on *#PosterChat*. By going legit we could certainly expand our reach. If we were to raise £5–10k (unlikely, but you never know), we could get billboards up across the country. We have no idea how much a legal poster costs (£1,000?), but it isn't beyond the realm of our collective imagination to have ten put up in towns and cities in the north.

On the other hand, this was never meant to be a legitimate advertising campaign. For us, the illegality of the

pasting is part of the reason we're doing it. Our side of the Brexit debate seems to us mired in technocratic (albeit important) assertions about jobs, rights and standards. What it lacks, we think, is passion. Where's the edge? We've taken our fair share of direct action over the years, be it against the Iraq War or climate change. We've scaled buildings and occupied headquarters, hung banners and even been arrested and prosecuted. Now Britain faces the single biggest political moment in its post-war history, the nation has cleaved in two and the debate is as brutalizing as anything we've experienced. A band of charlatans and frauds is on the verge of taking us out of Europe, based on a vote that was swung by lies and corruption. And yet nobody is so much as sitting down in the road.

No, the fact that we're breaking the law to put up our posters is, in a way, the whole *point* of the project.

And anyway we assume you have to publish your identity when you set up a crowdfunder, and we want to stay anonymous. We've committed multiple acts of criminal damage, and although we'd all happily take a criminal conviction in exchange for getting those seven posters up, none of us can afford a fine of many thousands of pounds or the burden of fifty hours' community service.

The next day *The Times* runs a double-page spread on our billboards. Davis, Fox and Rees-Mogg are called by journalists to account for their quotes. Yet more examples of fantasy and hypocrisy are flooding in from the public. Then we're messaged by the people at crowdfunder.co.uk. *Give us a call*, they say.

'We think your project could really work,' says Simon, the founder of the site. 'You could raise a bit of money.'

'We'd prefer to stay anonymous,' says James. 'Is that possible?'

'Of course. Why not start out asking for ten thousand, see how it goes?'

We're still not sure. But then we're sent a film from the *Kent Messenger* newspaper website, showing our posters being ripped down by Clear Channel – the company that

owns the sites in Dover. The footage includes a shot of the Rees-Mogg billboard being picked at and peeled off by a guy up a ladder. A 6 x 3m sheet of shite comes away from the board and crumples to the ground.

All that effort, and it stayed up for less than a day. We jump onto a Skype call.

'I think we should call the guys at Crowdfunder and tell them we'll do it,' says James.

'Let's do it,' says Will.

'Time to go legit,' says Olly.

'Like Al Pacino in *The Godfather Part II*,' says Ben.

Less than forty-eight hours after we trespassed on a platform overlooking an MOT centre in Dover, we resolve to become a legitimate campaign organization. We quickly agree on the £10k target and at 7 a.m. the next morning we go live.

> **James**: 300 quid ALREADY

> **Ben**: In first 3 minutes

> **James**: Guys this is going to go nuts

> **Olly**: Now £659!

> **James**: The money is coming in faster than likes/RTs/follows

> **Olly**: This is insane!

> **James**: Average donation 28 quid

Later...

> **Ben**: Just hit our target in 3 hours

> **Will:** Rio here we come!

> **Will:** (joke)

We sit at our computers – Ben and Olly in London, James in Bristol, Will in Sweden – staring at the screen, pressing *refresh*, watching the totalizer rolling over and over. By the end of the first day the crowdfunder has raised £30k and by the following evening we have £56k in the bank. We're now buyers in the cut-throat world of outdoor overhead advertising. And we have precisely no idea what we're doing.

Where do you even buy a billboard? Do you just phone someone up and order it? The guys at Crowdfunder tell us they've worked in the past with JCDecaux, the biggest billboard company in the country. James calls them and says we want to spend tens of thousands of pounds hiring their poster sites. He briefly outlines the concept and the support we're getting from the public.

'Hmm, sounds fascinating,' their woman replies. 'Send over your designs.'

So we email her what we want to put up across the country. It takes her ten minutes to reply.

'Absolutely no way. Sorry, this is all too political for us.'

Too political? In the past they happily plastered UKIP posters up and down the country. But they won't be budged.

Ben calls Clear Channel – another of the big three billboard companies – and explains what we're trying to do with the campaign.

'Sounds great,' the account manager says. 'Really interesting project. Let's do it.'

But an hour or so later he calls back.

'It's not actually great news,' he says. 'The higher-ups won't green-light it. The problem is... erm...'

'Is it Dover?'

'It's Dover.'

'Because we stole your sites?'

'Because you stole our sites.'

'I mean, fair enough.'

'We think so, yes.'

Next we try Primesight – owner of the Cameron board – but it's the same story.

By now we have £65K in the bank and the fund is growing every minute. People are clamouring for posters in their region, in their city, in their town, in their street. They're throwing cash at us and we have absolutely no idea how to spend it. This has the potential to be a total disaster. Our very own LBDexit. Should we just give all the money back? Can you even do that?

But then we get a message from an independent billboard company called Airoutdoor. They love the project, they say. *Can we help? We mainly have sites in Yorkshire and the Midlands. Are you interested?* Yes, we are. We're very interested indeed.

Meanwhile Ben has been given the number for the CEO of Build, another independent billboard company, specializing in advertising for gigs and album releases. We're told they're the kind of edgy outsiders who might take our money. *Build*? Where does he know that name from? Argh! It was on the corner of the site in Clapton. We pasted David Davis over one of their boards.

'God, I'm really sorry,' says Ben to the CEO across the table in a London café. 'We didn't really look at who owned it. It wasn't deliberate.'

'Not a problem. We love it. You're doing something really interesting here. Let's get your posters up.'

By now we have twenty-one potential quotes to get on billboards. We decide to launch with twelve designs – eleven decided by a Twitter poll, plus one quote that for us is non-negotiable. It's going up, whatever the public thinks. But first we check in with the billboard companies.

'You're okay putting up the Boris one, right?' asks James after emailing them the design.

'We're not okay with putting that one up, no,' says our new friend at Airoutdoor.

'You won't put FUCK BUSINESS on a billboard?'

'I'm afraid not.'

'Even though he said it.'

'Yup.'

'What about F-star-star-K BUSINESS?'

'Nope.'

'F-star-star-star BUSINESS?'

'I'm really sorry.'

'Star-star-star-star BUSINESS?'

'It's still a no.'

'But that could mean anything. It could be any word.'

'It could only be one word. We're just not allowed to put stuff like that up. Regulations. I'm sorry.'

It's the same at Build. No-go for Boris. James breaks the news on *#PosterChat*. But we won't take no for an answer. The billboard regulators can star-star-star-star off.

> **Ben:** We're doing FUCK BUSINESS anyway. Surely. It's too good.

> **James:** One option is we get that up before we go legit?

> **Olly:** I think we do it then we say that's it, we're legal now

Later...

> **Ben:** I've found a site half a mile from the Jaguar Land Rover factory in Solihull, heading towards it. We could do FUCK BUSINESS there

> **James:** GENIUS!!

> **Will:** Whoop!

> **Olly:** Boom! Love it

And so it happens that on a Sunday evening Olly puts his kids to bed, straps the ladder back onto the roofrack of his car and heads north towards Birmingham to meet James for our last guerrilla posting operation.

If we were worried about standing out in Dover, we're even more worried about Solihull – not so much because it's another Leave-voting town, but because of the content of the billboard. Before getting the poster printed, we discussed whether we should asterisk the quote (the road we've chosen is on a school run), but in the end we decided that Johnson said it, so he should own it. Jaguar Land Rover is already laying off workers because of Brexit; if we drop the 'F' bomb on a billboard, it might spark a local conversation about the direction the former foreign secretary and his allies are taking the country in. But it's going to take at least half an hour to paste the final eight sheets, meaning we'll be up a ladder on a busy road in front of a billboard proclaiming the word 'FUCK'. As ever, we're prepared to get arrested on a Led By Donkeys operation,

but our preference is to paste up the poster and get out of there.

The solution emerges, inevitably, on *#PosterChat*. Can't we put it up from right to left? The issue would be the overlaps, but if we don't paste the very left-hand edge of each sheet, we can tuck the next one under it. Maybe it can be done. We decide to give it a go, priding ourselves on our willingness to push the boundaries of billboard science.

It's nearly midnight before Olly arrives at the arranged meeting point in Solihull. James and his brother in-law Pete, who've driven up from Bristol, have already been waiting for twenty minutes. Time to get to work. The site we've chosen is right next to a tunnel, it's not well lit and at this time of night the street is quiet. We park up around the corner, grab the gear and arrive at the site.

'Stop!' shouts Olly.

'What is it?' says James, looking round for a police car.

Olly takes his phone from his pocket and turns on the torch. For the next forty seconds he holds it about sixty

centimetres from the ground, sweeping the beam over the path below the billboard.

'All good, carry on.'

Some mistakes don't bear repetition.

It's another cold night and our hands ache with pain from being covered in freezing paste. But after half an hour the billboard is almost finished. The final incriminating sheets – Boris Johnson's face and the word *FUCK* – go up last. We stand back. It's a powerful poster for its simplicity, while the location so close to the car factory gives it real relevance. We think it captures Johnson's arrogance, his disregard for anything that stands in his way, his fundamental lack of concern for other people. But there's no time to dwell on it. We say our goodbyes and head for home. With long drives ahead, it will be after 3 a.m. before we're in bed.

The poster certainly sparks a local conversation. **Fury over giant 'f***' billboard ad posted on busy road near school,** runs the headline in the *Birmingham Mail*. The newspaper quotes various posts from the local residents' Facebook group. Lindsey Crompton has declared: 'I complained to the company who own the billboard who told me they knew nothing about it. They removed it within 2 hours. Apparently it was installed last night about 11 o'clock. What offends me is that these activists think it is okay to put such language on a billboard in a residential area. Utter disgrace by led by donkeys.' Pat Kennedy has written: 'I couldn't believe what I was seeing this morning... disgraceful.' James Hipwell has posted: 'Maybe these idiots should get a job and stop trying to be Twitter famous.'

But resident Emily McKenzie has responded, saying: 'I hope everyone outraged by the language used on this billboard because children will see it, was equally outraged when this statement was made by someone who literally shapes the future of those same children. If my children asked me what that statement meant, I'd tell them, and I'd tell them who said it and what his job was. In an ideal world the billboard wouldn't be there, but in an ideal world our foreign secretary wouldn't be the type of person who thinks "f***k

business" is an acceptable response to people losing their jobs.' And Chris Hammond has written: 'Yes, the expletive is unfortunate. But it's had an impact and got people talking.'

Which is the whole point of Led By Donkeys.

The day after posting Johnson, we launch the Twitter poll asking our followers – the people paying for the next phase of the campaign – which examples of Brexit bunkum they want pasted up now. When the results are in, Will gets busy turning the most popular into giant tweets. But then we're sent a clip from Jacob Rees-Mogg's LBC radio show.

Eduardo from Chigwell has called in. 'The question I have for you today,' he says to Rees-Mogg, 'is to do with your tweet in 2011 where you said, in your words, it might make more sense to have a second referendum after the renegotiation is completed. My question is why has your position changed?'

Rees-Mogg replies, 'Because I wasn't on Twitter in 2011, I only joined in 2017 so it would have been very remarkable if I had tweeted in 2011. Thank you so much for your point.'

Fake news! screams Brexit Twitter. *The quote is faked!*

It isn't, of course. Rees-Mogg said it in the House of Commons. But the incident makes us stop and think for a moment. We're no longer just a fly-posting crew going out at night to satisfy our own frustrations. We're now a national campaign – a minor player in the most brutally contested political fight in post-war British history – with pictures of our billboards going viral every time we post one. There's now less room for the no-holds-barred guerrilla sensibility that's guided us this far.

Will adds a caveat to the posters. So, for example, Gove's *we hold all the cards* now includes a source in the bottom-left corner: *He didn't tweet it, he actually said it! In a speech at Vote Leave HQ.*

We send our designs over to the billboard companies, and just ten days after we set up the crowdfunder, Led By Donkeys' posters are poised to go up on twenty-eight sites across Yorkshire, the Midlands, Bristol and London.

We're going legit.

28 January–28 February 2019 ✔

@ByDonkeys

Launch day. We're excited but a little nervous, far from certain that anybody will even care. It's been nearly two weeks since we last put up a poster – an epoch in Twitter time – and we wonder if our concept is about to fall foul of the law of diminishing returns. Will people be interested in a suite of new billboards? And will the fact that they were legally posted mean our project has lost its edge and, with it, the interest of our followers? By now we're on multiple social-media platforms, so we divide up responsibility for the channels, with Ben taking Twitter, James doing Facebook and Olly covering Instagram (and Will designing all our content, without which we'd have nothing to post). But what if we're now the digital equivalent of yesterday's chip-wrapping?

At 7.30 a.m. on 28 January, Ben hesitantly presses *send* on the first tweet of our national campaign:

> ⚪ BOOM! We're throwing their exact words back at them. Our UK-wide ad campaign – paid for by you – just launched in Leeds (50/50 in ref). Many more places to follow. We're turning Brexiteer quotes into tweets & slapping them on billboards. #LedByDonkeys

A few minutes later we check in on *#PosterChat*.

> **Ben**: We're live. Let's see if anyone notices

Will: 👊

Olly: The meters are clicking away!

James: We have a national billboard campaign. Wtf?

Ben: Already getting hassled by TV

Will: It's working. People still like it

Olly: Phew

Not for the first time we're a little stunned by the impact Led By Donkeys is having. We started it as a modest project to do something purgative for ourselves, thinking we'd maybe reach a few Leavers while we were at it, but now we've raised something close to £80k, we have 36k followers (more than Raab) and a backlog of interview requests from UK and international media.

How did this happen? What the hell is going on here?

Key to the success of the project, we decide, is the simplicity of the concept. All we're doing is putting up the words of the Brexiters and letting the public do the rest. No commentary from us, just historic quotes and an implicit request that the words be compared to the reader's observed reality. Some of the quotes did the rounds online weeks or months ago, but they never seemed to stick. Content is ephemeral in the age of social media, but by taking the quotes and pasting them in town centres, we're giving them an impact that's hard to achieve online. On Twitter and Facebook the quotes circulated in a bubble of like-minded people who vented for a few minutes before their outrage found a new focus. A tweet, with its rounded corners, circular thumbnail images and heart-shaped buttons is designed for the

age of distraction. The mighty billboard, on the other hand, is pretty much its antithesis – a giant splintering plywood plinth, built to be pasted with countless layers of blue-backed paper. It glares down at you, unchanging and immune to your finger jabs. While your phone screen refreshes sixty times a second and there is an infinite number of alternative pages to distract you, to move you on, an old-school billboard changes only once every two weeks. So by being physically posted in public spaces, the quotes finally actually exist, drawing significance and relevance from the fact that everyone – no matter their take on Brexit – is exposed to them. In villages, towns and cities across the UK a small piece of political street theatre is being performed all day every day, in front of people of every political persuasion.

You can't have a billboard in a bubble.

Then, by photographing our posters and playing the images back into the digital world, they come alive online, with explosive effect. It's accidental alchemy.

But perhaps more than anything, we're satisfying a deep need amongst many hundreds of thousands, maybe even millions, of people to right what they feel is a fundamental wrong. Our followers and funders might not be up a ladder covered in wallpaper paste, but it's their donations that are now putting those posters up. They're chipping in at their desks at work or throwing us a few quid on their phones while riding the bus home. We're being inundated with messages from people around the country, saying things like: *It's great to finally see someone sticking it back to them* and *This is the best £20 I've ever spent* and *I wish I could give you more but it's a few days till pay day, but here's a fiver*. It's those donations – the ones of two, three, five pounds – that we find truly humbling. They're from people who can't afford to give much, but who have nevertheless put their faith in us.

In the days after we launch, we raise more money than we imagined was possible. The crowdfunder pot hits £90k, then £100k. We all feel uncomfortable sitting on that much

cash while remaining anonymous. Politics on both sides of the Atlantic is being corrupted by dark money – the injection of huge sums of undeclared corporate cash into operations by fake think tanks to slow action on, for example, climate change and tax avoidance. It's a scourge we've long battled in our day jobs. We know we're a genuine grassroots outfit, but how can people be sure we're not the creation of a powerful interest group? We rationalize it all by reminding ourselves that we're funded by the public, and anyway the project will soon burn out and nobody will care.

But a week later we're still here. We beat Steve Baker for Twitter followers, then Arron Banks. David Davis claims we've taken him out of context. Liam Fox's office issues an incoherent quote, claiming he's being misrepresented. Rees-Mogg vents to his local paper, the *Bristol Post*, about a Donkeys billboard that we've put up in the city, calling it 'fundamentally dishonest' (it's not).

When we post our response to him with a picture of the poster, it gets 14k retweets and is seen 1.5 million times in people's timelines. We've taken a quote, turned it into a tweet, put it on a billboard, tweeted a photo of that billboard, the tweet's gone viral, the local newspaper's written about the viral tweet of a billboard of a tweet, that article itself has gone viral, then our tweet about the article has exploded. It's a kind of meta-virality that we struggle to get our heads round. All we know for sure is that we're in a scrap with the leading Brexiters – the people who broke our hearts back in 2016, the politicians seeking to amputate our European identities against our will. They're finally being forced to answer for what they said, and it feels wonderful.

Where previously we woke in the morning and scrolled through the latest Brexit news only to feel immediate dejection, now the first thing we do each day is check *#PosterChat*. Olly's partner asks him what he thinks of the latest Johnson atrocity and, with joy in his heart, he tells her he hasn't even heard about it because he's been too busy booking billboard space. Far from feeling like work, the Donkeys project is a powerful tonic that forces us to shed

the sense of hopeless frustration that comes with being a Remainer in Brexit Britain. We're actually *doing* something, and we're doing it together, four friends who each bring something different to the team. This must be what it feels like being in a half-decent band, playing packed-out gigs. And the reviews so far are pretty good. The expected wave of online abuse is yet to materialize, while the love for Donkeys is a little overwhelming.

On a Saturday afternoon Ben is scrolling through the mentions on Twitter when he reads a tweet, squints, reads it again and bursts out laughing. He calls James.

'Hey, man,' says James.

'Can you talk?'

'I'm driving, but I'm on hands-free. What's up?'

'Okay, I want to tell you something, but try not to lose control of the car and crash.'

'Oh God, what's happened? Have we messed up?'

'No, no, I've just read a tweet by a PR guy. He's at the Munich Security Conference and he says Tony Blair's there, and Blair is making a speech and he's given a big shout-out to Led by Donkeys.'

'No way! That's hilarious. What did he say?'

'Apparently we're the smart new way to fight populism.'

'Ha!'

'Right,' says Ben.

'Hang on,' says James, 'didn't you once help organize a blockade of a military base to stop weapons being sent to Iraq?'

'Yeah. Olly got nicked on that one, when he locked himself Inside a tank. And weren't you once on the BBC for heckling Blair about Iraq?'

'That's right, yeah.'

'Awkward.'

We're running this thing in the gaps between our day jobs and kids. From 6 a.m. the four of us plot out the day on *#PosterChat* until we're interrupted by baby monitors or children demanding breakfast. We're authorizing ad

spends of £20,000 or £30,000 while pushing a pram to nursery; new posters are signed off by tapping on our phones under the table in meetings at work; we discreetly message about new billboard designs on phones tucked between cushions, while supposedly watching films with our partners; ideas to expose the Brexit bullshit are being developed in supermarket aisles, children's playgrounds, cartoon screenings at cinemas and up hills on long country walks at the weekend. After 10 p.m. when our kids and partners have gone to bed we're back on *#PosterChat* deciding what to do the next morning. It's anarchic, but the dynamic between us means ideas get rounded up – language is tightened, designs improved, strategy ever more focused. It's a long way from the necessarily more complicated (and, for us, familiar) process of making decisions in a big organization. And it's all possible because our partners are supporters of the project. They bear the weight of our distraction. Without them, it wouldn't be happening.

By now Led By Donkeys is meta-sizing, and running this thing is becoming more complex with every passing day. Britain's billboards are updated every fortnight, meaning that we have to book more spots to keep the campaign visible. Two weeks after our launch we're about to go up on forty more sites, but before pressing the button on the next phase of posters we discuss whether we should pull some of the designs. We've come in for some stick from a couple of London-based commentators, who say optimistic quotes such as Gove's *we hold all the cards* will be taken literally by Leave voters, who'll assume our billboards are part of a pro-Brexit campaign. Our critics say the irony will be lost on them. We get messages from Remainer dudes (they're always men) saying; *This is the biggest self-own I've ever seen* and *If this is symptomatic of what the next Remain campaign is going to be like, we've lost already.*

Will is touring the country photographing billboards. He speaks to people interacting with the posters and checks their reaction – our own shoestring focus groups – and finds

that the great British public is sharp enough to understand what we're doing. Many might not agree with us, but they get the point. Moreover the posters' real impact is coming from the media coverage they're attracting. More often than not, a billboard becomes a local news story, and those articles are consistently the most viewed and commented-upon stories on news websites up and down the country. They usually include a quote from us or other anti-Brexit campaigners, and rack up thousands of shares and likes on Facebook groups where the real Brexit debate is playing out. In those stories, at least, the debate is being conducted on our terms, with the focus on the gulf between the historic statements of leading Brexiters and what they're saying now. It's precisely the effect we hoped the posters would have.

We keep Gove's cards and Fox's trade deal in our repertoire.

It's 6 a.m. on a Wednesday morning just four weeks after Cameron went up and we're meeting Al Jazeera, the *Guardian* and US radio network NPR in front of a billboard in west London. They want to see one being pasted up and to interview us about the campaign. But they don't know who we are. Nobody does. We started out being anonymous because we were breaking the law, and we've kept it that way, not wanting to be arrested now for past crimes. But anonymity also works for the project. We want the posters to speak for themselves, unencumbered by a conversation about who put them there. In this digital age people are so used to focusing on the messenger. *Do they look like me? Whose side are they on?* We think the politicians' words have more power when publicized by unnamed individuals. And when the first death-threat comes in, that seals it: we're keeping our names out of this. So, we give the journalists pseudonyms – Olly becomes Adam, Ben is Richard and James goes for Chris. (Will can't make the interview.)

We watch with boyish admiration as Dave – the professional poster-paster who's plastering our London billboards – gets Rees-Mogg up in under twenty minutes. It's the first

time we've observed an expert put up a poster. He is a master of his craft, who manoeuvres and manipulates the paper with a one-handed wire brush, so that instead of ending up with sheets wrapped around his head and wallpaper paste dripping from his nose, he controls the sheets in much the same way a snooker player directs a cue ball. He can place it exactly where he wants with a barely perceptible touch. We stare up in wonder, like kids on a football terrace watching a star striker warm up. None of the techniques and modifications we developed on *#PosterChat* come close to this.

Then Dave finishes sheet twelve, climbs down the ladder and is approached by the journalists for his take on our project, whereupon he announces that he's a Leaver. The hacks scribble down his words enthusiastically. *Oh Christ*, we think, *the headline writes itself. FIFTH DONKEY IS A BREXITER*. But when it appears a few days later, the *Guardian*'s write-up is an affectionate account of the project that further boosts our profile. The article gets 120k likes, comments and shares on Facebook, we're flooded with donations and our Twitter follower-count passes 50k, taking out Nadine Dorries and John Redwood. Two weeks after that, we're up on another seventy billboard sites.

One effect we hadn't predicted – something intangible but nevertheless priceless – is the morale boost that the proliferation of the billboards seems to be giving to people who voted Remain in the referendum. Since June 2016 we've been branded 'saboteurs' and 'citizens of nowhere' by a Brexit political and media establishment that's acted like it won the referendum 80/20. But from the messages we receive from around the country it's evident that, for many people, the posters are having an energizing effect. One of our followers – a Brit living in Amsterdam – builds an online map of all our poster locations, and it's only when we open it that we truly grasp how big this thing has become. Half of Britain is covered in Donkeys posters.

We're interviewed by national newspapers and magazines from Spain, Portugal, Greece, Holland and

Germany. We know we won't persuade many Leave voters to change their minds by getting coverage in the *Frankfurter Allgemeine Zeitung*, but we want to tell Europe a different story about Britain. Right now it's the Brexit ultras of the European Research Group (ERG) appearing on TV screens across the world, but they don't represent the country and culture that we're proud to be a part of. It pains us to think of these monomaniacal oddballs and xenophobes claiming to speak for Britain. The concept of Led By Donkeys relies on a very British sense of humour and we want Europeans to see a bit of that spirit. So we make time for the foreign media.

Meanwhile the British tabloid press, dominated as it is by a cultish adherence to the pro-Brexit line, studiously ignores our very existence. Their journalists follow us on Twitter, but they won't write a word about us. That's okay; the tweets have appeared in local newspapers from Glasgow to Portsmouth, so we don't need the tabloids. We've rinsed Johnson, Gove, Raab, Davis, Farage and half a dozen other leading Brexiters and our posters have been seen by millions of people.

But what about Corbyn? What do we say about Jez? Should he get the Donkeys treatment? He's a Brexiter, right? Or is he? What does he actually think? Back in The Birdcage, we hold a strategy meeting to decide our approach towards the Labour leader. James opens his laptop and says he has an idea for a Corbyn poster, then spins his computer round. We stare at the screen, then all crack up, laughing. A tweet by @JeremyCorbyn. But it's blank. There's nothing there.

We pay to have it go up on a board in his constituency, opposite the Arsenal stadium. A couple of days before it's pasted, we tip off For our Future's Sake (FFS) — an anti-Brexit youth group with many Labour members — and invite them to come down and write on the poster what they want Corbyn *actually* to say on Brexit. The morning it goes up, we chain a stepladder to the billboard, leave three spray cans and retreat across the road to watch events unfold. The activists arrive, with a media scrum in tow.

A young woman climbs the ladder and sprays *PEOPLE'S VOTE!!* Another young woman sprays *Love Jez H8 Brexit* on the blank Corbyn tweet. An elderly pedestrian stops, asks what's going on and a moment later is climbing the ladder to write his own message. The stunt is on that evening's *BBC News at Ten* (it will later be on the front of the *Financial Times* and in *The New York Times*).

But the next day Islington Council orders the poster to be covered up. They say it's graffiti. We're perplexed: we paid for the poster, the billboard company gave us permission to scribble on it. Not to be deterred, Will sources a press photograph of the defaced poster, then on his laptop he mounts it in the kind of ornate gold frame more often seen in galleries. We get this new design printed out and pasted on the same site in Islington.

Is it art? Who knows? But it's definitely not graffiti any more, because it's allowed to stay up.

By now our content has appeared more than forty million times on people's Twitter timelines, Facebook feeds and Instagram accounts. Our social-media impact is beyond anything we imagined possible when we started this thing, but because we're working with just two small billboard companies we can only access a limited number of sites, meaning that our geographical reach is limited. We're messaged by people in Devon, Cornwall, Norfolk, Northern Ireland and every other corner of the country where we've not put up posters. People wonder why they haven't had a Donkeys billboard near them. They assume we've made a conscious decision to ignore them.

We need to make peace with the market leaders in the billboard world – the companies that shunned us a few weeks back. One of our followers has sent us the email address of a senior manager at Clear Channel, and we send him a grovelling email offering to compensate them for lost earnings from the guerrilla boards in Dover. A few hours later James gets a call to his burner phone (we're all using pay-as-you-go SIM cards in old handsets for Donkeys work) and after a short but intense bollocking, he's informed that

Clear Channel is now prepared to reverse its decision and take our money.

We're excited by the opportunities this presents, but also conflicted. None of us are fans of the way our local landscapes have been taken over by billboards imploring us to buy things we don't need, and now we're doing business with one of the goliaths of the industry. We rationalize it by telling ourselves that every billboard we get up means one less advert for something we don't need that goes straight to landfill.

By getting Clear Channel involved, we now have access to the whole country. We can also get our posters up on a suite of giant 12 x 3m billboards that we've wanted to get our hands on since we first went legit. By using double-sized boards we can run two tweets side-by-side, allowing us to do a compare-and-contrast between the Brexiters' contradictory statements. And we're particularly excited about pasting up a double Michael Gove.

Clear Channel promises us a site outside Billingsgate fish market in London. Given the content of the two quotes we're going to put next to each other, it's the perfect location. A few weeks later, when we hear it's finally up, Ben pockets his camera and takes the Docklands Light Railway down to the site. *This one's going to be good*, he's thinking. *Well worth the wait*. He walks along the busy dual carriageway in the shadow of Canary Wharf's skyscrapers. Up ahead he can see the familiar black-on-white of a Donkeys billboard. And it's huge. What a coup. As he arrives, he looks up and reads the board. And his stomach sinks.

You know when you write the perfect tweet and you post it and you're so damn proud of yourself, but when you go back and look at it, you see that you've spelled a word wrong and it really pisses you off? Well, when you put up a 36 sq/m billboard on one of the busiest roads in London and you spot a typo, it absolutely kills you. It may only be one stray letter, but we've become obsessive about the project. Perfectionists even.

One the left side is Gove during the referendum campaign in 2016: *The one thing which will not change is our ability to trade freely with Europe.* And on the right side, in huge letters hanging above Ben's head, is a Gove quote from 2019: *There is no absolute gaurantee that we would be able to continue to export food to the EU.*

'Gaurantee.'

The pain is deep and searing.

As each new fortnightly wave of posters is about to go up, Ben tells the team that this will be his last, that he has to devote himself fully to his daughter and his pregnant girlfriend. He knows he's been a less-than-perfect partner these past two months, but he tells himself he's doing it for his kids' future. Olly tells himself the same thing. He's struggling to juggle the project with overseas work trips and, when he is at home, he finds he's glued to his phone. His two daughters note his mental absence and suggest they install a box by the front door, into which Olly would drop his phone when he gets home each evening, but it never happens. One night his partner comes to bed to find him sitting with his laptop open, staring at a picture of Nigel Farage. 'Research,' he says feebly. She pulls the duvet up to her chin, rolls over and sighs. Will, meanwhile, is doing much of the design work after midnight, in a vain effort to keep his freelance photography career on the tracks, but that means he's often exhausted by the time he's feeding his children breakfast. And James is also sacrificing freelance income, so now his family is dipping deep into the fund set aside to redo the bathroom.

This is not sustainable and it's not fair on our families, but we're loath to call time on the project. Our fourth series of posters has just gone up on eighty sites, we've raised more than £200k, we have 80k twitter followers and we can see from local media reports that almost every new billboard is sparking a conversation between Leavers and Remainers. We all know how rare it is to have a campaign

take off like this. It's like catching lightning in a jam jar.

The question of Led By Donkeys' continued existence is finally resolved when Nigel Farage announces an 'epic protest march' from Sunderland to Parliament Square. He's billing the walk as a modern-day incarnation of the Jarrow March, an uprising against the elites, when in reality it's being bankrolled by multimillionaire property tycoon Richard Tice.

No, we're not shutting down. Not now. No way.

Farage has registered MarchToLeave.com, but has neglected to buy the more patriotic version of his website. One of our followers jumps on MarchToLeave.co.uk, registers it and messages us to ask if we can do anything with it. We scrape the Brexiters' website and copy it wholesale onto our own version, then start amending it. The event is renamed MARCH TO LEAVE BRITAIN IF BREXIT IS A DISASTER, in recognition of Farage's promise to do just that. On the page detailing the route we amend the stops, so that the protesters pass through each of the six constituencies where Farage failed to win election to Westminster. Now leg one is from Brussels to Bexhill, while leg three is from Eastleigh to Salisbury, where *the marchers will take in the famous spire of Salisbury Cathedral and later join Nigel for an evening discussion on the geo-politics of Brexit, in which he will elaborate on his assertion that the world leader he most admires is Vladimir Putin. The town is the site of a strong 1997 electoral performance in which Nigel polled 5.7% and kept his deposit.*

We launch the site with a new crowdfunder – a target to raise £30k in four days to pay for two digital ad-vans to accompany every mile of the march (it's something of a surprise when our spoof site and ad-van idea are covered favourably by the *Express* and the *Telegraph*). Our plan is to display Farage's most egregious hypocrisies and fantasies on the vans' 8 sq/m display boards and have them crawl along the road beside him and his followers. We want to spark a conversation among his supporters about who this man really is, and we're hoping to influence media coverage of the march. Too often Farage gets a clear run, we think. Even on the BBC.

But will people stump up the cash for us to do it? Once again we're overwhelmed with donations and humbled by how quickly we raise the money. We book the ad-vans and Will comes over from Sweden to run the launch operation. He grew up in Widdrington, just north of Newcastle, and knows the area well. The march is scheduled to begin on a Saturday morning, but nobody beyond Farage's top team knows where the starting point is, not even the marchers themselves. It feels like we've scored an early victory when a journalist tells us that Farage's people are saying the secrecy is because they're worried about our ad-vans.

Will wakes at 4.30 a.m. at his parents' house near the Scottish border, groggy with the particular anxiety that comes from having a big day ahead but having barely slept. He inhales coffee and cornflakes, then steps out into a snowstorm, goes back inside to put on more layers, then clambers into his car and heads south towards Sunderland.

The A1 is covered in a thick blanket of white, and it feels like he's going so slowly he might as well be pushing the damn car. Every half-hour the radio news bulletin mentions Farage and the first day of the March to Leave, and Will feels a stab of fear that he won't get there on time. And even if he does, he won't know where the march is setting off from.

By the time he passes Newcastle the snow has turned to slush and Will's nerves are thawing. He's going to make it. As he pulls into Sunderland the rain is beating on the bonnet of his car. There's an hour before the march is due to start and he's hoping to snap some of the Farage billboards we've had put up overnight. He's in the city centre photographing a jacked-up Range Rover under a giant tweet, when his phone pings with a message from a contact in the media.

Ryhope – The Hendon Grange Pub.

So that's where Farage is starting from.

Will checks his map. It's by a roundabout less than a hundred metres up the road from a giant 36 sq/m double

billboard that's perfect for Sunderland, home of the Nissan factory. Before long he's circling the roundabout, craning his neck to read the billboard. On the left side is Farage's Leave.EU campaign from 2016: *Project Fear claims Nissan would scale back UK operation could not have been further from the truth! #BrexitBritain*. On the right side is a Sky News tweet from last month: *Japanese car-maker Nissan is cancelling plans to build its X-Trail model at its plant in Sunderland*.

An outside-broadcast van is parked under the poster, while a car with a *Leave means Leave* poster in the window is crawling along the verge. It pulls up, the driver gets out and stares up at the billboard, then slams the car door closed, shaking his head. Will turns off the roundabout and heads down a narrow road towards the pub, where he parks up in front of a police car.

It's too quiet. Where is everyone? Will gets out and looks around. A flag-waving couple is disappearing down an alleyway, so he follows them and a minute later the track comes out into a field behind the pub. And Will gets his first sight of the March to Leave.

He's looking out on a litter-strewn wasteland with some 200 marchers milling about in a shower of horizontal rain. Camera crews and pro-EU counter-protesters stand on the edge of the gathering, watching the marchers. A young woman lets off two flares and shouts something as blue-and-yellow smoke pours into the air, then quickly blows into the crowd, swirling around the wet anoraks and Brexit placards. To her right a scuffle breaks out, but a moment later the protagonists think better of it and step back. Will lifts his video camera, turns it onto the scene and shoots a twenty-second film. He uploads it to *#PosterChat*.

Will: Here it is. The March To Leave

Olly: Ha! Wow

> **Ben:** God this is going to be fun

His film shows a bleak, sparsely populated gathering that is utterly at odds with the spectacular moment promised by Farage and the Brexit newspapers. Two minutes later Ben has tweeted it out with the message:

> ⬤ Hi millionaire elite property tycoon and Farage funder @TiceRichard, is this the 'epic protest march' you've been talking about? Cos right now there are more people in the queue at my local Tesco #MarchToLeave #EpicProtestMarch

The video goes viral in minutes. 20,000, 30,000, 50,000, 100,000 views. Over the course of the day it will reach 700,000. Our hope is that the film makes it more difficult for the media to present the launch as a success and, judging from the change in tone of the online coverage, it does just that.

As the marchers set off along the clifftop coastal path, Will jumps into his car and races ahead. A few miles down the road he spots a car park next to the path, pulls over and calls in the ad-vans. Ten minutes later they're in position, the LED-screens' brightness set to full. Behind him Will hears a rumbling, spluttering engine and in the rear-view mirror he sees an open-top double-decker bus emblazoned with the March to Leave logo. It parks up, before stewards decamp and stand around chatting. It seems they're planning a short rally here in the car park. A few minutes later Farage appears, leading a thinned-out crowd of already bedraggled marchers. Will gets out of the car and sets up his camera on a tripod. Farage looks around and spots the two screens scrolling through his quotes, glances at Will, bites his lip and attempts a forced conversation with the man walking next to him, but that guy has also spotted the screens and he's stopped to read them. Farage carries

on alone. As he passes Will, he turns his head and the two of them stare at each other for a moment. Behind Farage's head one of the screens flashes with a new message: *If Brexit is a disaster I will go and live abroad, I'll go and live somewhere else.*

'Oh, there's the EU-funded billboards,' shouts one of the marchers.

'Paid for by Soros,' shouts another.

Farage steps onto the bus and a moment later emerges on the top deck, standing at the back, diminished and alone. Below him a small ragtag band of soaked men stare up in silence. A discarded placard is floating in a puddle. Will's heart is thumping hard now; he knows this is a moment of supreme political theatre. He fishes his phone from his pocket and calls the ad-van drivers, telling them to move so that the screens are facing the bus, and as the vans' engines start he raises his video camera. One of the ad-vans reverses and the words *We need to move to an insurance-based system of healthcare* crawl into Farage's line of sight. He glances down from the top of the bus. His supporters turn and read the screen. Farage grimaces and drums his fingers on the seat in front, then stares into the middle distance, his expression one of baffled defeat.

Gotcha.

Will uploads the film to *#PosterChat*, then we edit it so that it ends by slowly closing in on Farage's face to capture in close-up the precise moment it dawns on him that he is the author of an omnishambles. Over the top we add a haunting piano melody. The film closes with the words: *Sorry nobody turned up for your 'epic protest march' Nigel. Love Led By Donkeys x*

It will be viewed more than two million times.

The next morning Will is up early to position his camera in a car park on the outskirts of Hartlepool, the starting point for leg two. The promised crowd of thousands is again absent, but so is the media. Fearing Farage will claim a huge turnout, Will flies a drone above the marchers and films

them setting off, then watches the footage back, counting their numbers. There are seventy-seven of them and no sign of Farage or Tice. The March to Leave is a numerically imploding farce.

'Where's Nigel today?' Will calls out. 'Is he coming?'

'No, he's got his LBC show today,' comes the loyal reply.

The marchers have been abandoned. They paid £50 each to be part of an inspiring, huge two-week rally across the country, but now they're a sparse band, trudging leaderless towards Middlesbrough as their talisman prioritizes his radio phone-in show.

It would be easy to ridicule the marchers, but we think better of it. We may disagree with them but, as activists ourselves, we have respect for anybody who makes sacrifices to make their point peacefully, and that includes Farage's followers. No, our contempt is reserved for the elite taxpayer-funded media insider who conceived this farce, then did a runner as soon as the cameras left. We created Led By Donkeys to expose the lies of the Brexit leaders,

not to target normal people expressing their beliefs. Sure, they're Brexiters, but we all have people in our lives who voted Leave and we love them dearly. Those marchers could be our grandpas, uncles or close family friends.

It looks, to us, as if an opportunist politician has conceived a scheme that was undeliverable. He persuaded members of the public to make sacrifices to further it and recruited millionaires to bankroll it, and when it failed he simply walked away. The March to Leave is just a fourteen-day metaphor for Brexit.

Olly: A quite sad but big chat broke out on Instagram about this woman who was proud of her husband for marching in the rain. She said people should stop taking the piss out of him. I said she was right to be proud of him, marching for something he believed in, and that our criticism is of Farage and the Brexit leaders, not the people who voted for it. So I think the scale issue is out there and we need to keep it on Farage

James: Had exactly the same exchange on Facebook and said the same

Ben: We need to punch up, not down

Will: 100%

James: Reckon we should dial back to 1 ad-van potentially after today. Let's discuss later but if you think 2 is overkill today we could always tell one to go home early. Don't want to seem like the Goliath here

Will: Need to keep it on Farage

Despite resolving to show the marchers the respect we feel they deserve, our approach is not always reciprocated. One marcher tries to wrestle Will's camera tripod away from him, another repeatedly stands in front of his camera chanting, 'Leave means Leave!'

'Why do you feel like you have to cover up Nigel's words?' asks Will. 'You know we're not trying to belittle you or attack you. We're not doing anything to disrespect you here. We're just putting the things he said back into a public space.'

The guy stands silently and aggressively, staring into Will's face, holding a Brexit placard, blocking the camera, refusing to engage.

In the late afternoon the marchers trudge into Middlesbrough. One of them waves a huge British flag as they pass underneath a Donkeys billboard we've placed on the route. It's a 2016 quote from a group of right-wing academics calling itself Economists for Brexit: *Over time, if we left the EU, it seems likely that we would mostly eliminate manufacturing... But this shouldn't scare us.*

Brexit encapsulated.

It's a coup to get the shot, but instead of exhilaration, Will feels empty. It's been a long weekend and he's spent

it soaking and cold, wading through bile and hatred. It didn't take long for the marchers to realize he was organizing the Led By Donkeys vans and soon enough he was being bombarded with insults and provocations. It's been emotionally exhausting. But worst of all has been the reductionist simplicity of the slogan *Leave means Leave*. It's been shouted at him dozens of times, held on banners in front of his face, spat into the microphone by Farage from atop his bus. They've levelled it at him like a universal truth that cannot be denied, and the experience has left Will feeling more pessimistic than ever about the prospects of an easing of tensions between Britain's warring political tribes. The slogan is Brexit condensed into a verbal brawl, a football chant; it means absolutely nothing, but it's all its proponents have to offer this region. Will's relieved that he's only following the march for the weekend and not the whole fortnight. He doesn't think he could tolerate hearing that damn slogan even one more time.

That night he takes the long road home. He needs time to process what he's feeling, so he phones his parents to say he's going to be late. They moved to a town on the Scottish border when he was thirteen, but now Will feels the need to go back to the place where he grew up. He hasn't seen it for more than a decade, but he finds himself pulling up outside the boys' club in Widdrington where he played football when he was a kid. He gets out of the car and runs a hand along the wall, like he used to do when he was at primary school here. He's been on the end of so much hate, and all he wants to do is reconnect with his childhood, with happy memories, with love and pride for the north-east.

He sits on the wall and bursts into tears.

Sunderland, Tyne and Wear – 16 March 2019 (Photograph: Will Rose)

Castlebank Street, Glasgow – 23 March 2019 (Photograph: Jeremy Sutton-Hibbert)

Purewell Cross / Somerford Road, Christchurch, Dorset – 15 March 2019 (Photograph: Luke MacGregor)

Notts County FC, Cattle Market Road, Nottingham – 16 February 2019 (Photograph: Fionn Guilfoyle)

Rochdale, Greater Manchester – 19 March 2019 (Photograph: Jon Super)

Parkfield Road, Wolverhampton, Staffordshire — 21 February 2019 (Photograph: Will Rose)

Boulevard Anspach / Place de Brouckère, Brussels – 20 February 2019 (Photograph: Frédéric Moreau)

Westminster Bridge Road, central London — 4 March 2019 (Photograph: Will Rose)

Trinity Way, West Bromwich, West Midlands – 8 March 2019 (Photograph: iD8 Photography)

Cricklewood Broadway, London – 7 March 2019 (Photograph: Chris J. Ratcliffe)

Chain Bridge Road, Newcastle City Centre – 10 March 2019 (Photograph: Will Rose)

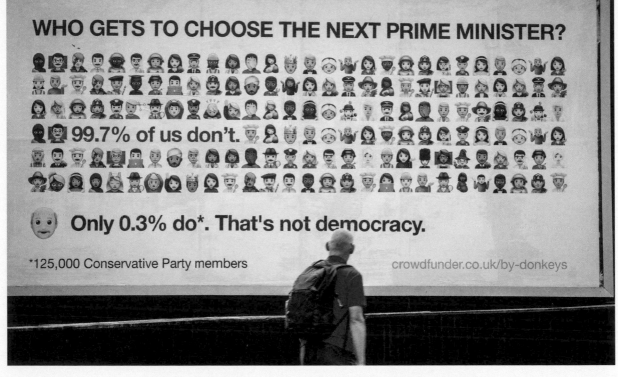

WHO GETS TO CHOOSE THE NEXT PRIME MINISTER?

99.7% of us don't.

Only 0.3% do*. That's not democracy.

*125,000 Conservative Party members

crowdfunder.co.uk/by-donkeys

Abbotsbury Road, Weymouth, Dorset — 24 June 2019 (Photograph: Luke MacGregor)

West India Dock Road, Canary Wharf, London – 16 April 2019
(Photograph: Suzanne Plunkett)

Liverpool Road, Cadishead, Manchester – 24 February 2019 (Photograph: Will Rose)

Molesworth Street, Rochdale, Greater Manchester – 19 March 2019
(Photograph: Jon Super)

Arsenal, London – 11 April 2019 (Photograph: Chris J. Ratcliffe)

Park Road McDonald's, Halesowen, West Midlands – 9 March 2019
(Photograph: Matt Wright)

Tottenham Lane / Church Lane, Hornsey, London – 15 April 2019 (Photograph: Will Rose)

Lower Cathedral Road, Cardiff – 1 March 2019 (Photograph:4Pi)

Commercial Road, Leeds – 28 January 2019 (Photograph: Steve Morgan)

London Road, London – 11 April 2019 (Photograph: Chris J. Ratcliffe)

Wick Road, Hackney, London – 15 March 2019 (Photograph: Suzanne Plunket)

Liverpool Road, Irlam, Manchester – 24 February 2019 (Photograph: Will Rose)

Wellington Street, Stockport, Greater Manchester – 24 February 2019 (Photograph: Will Rose)

Cricklewood Broadway, London – 13 March 2019 (Photograph: Suzanne Plunkett)

Bolton Road, Anderton, Lancashire – 23 February 2019 (Photograph: Will Rose)

Woolwich Road, Greenwich, London – 2 June 2019 (Photograph: Luke MacGregor)

Egerton Street, Bolton, Greater Manchester – 23 June 2019 (Photograph: Dean Atkins)

18–23 March 2019 ✓
@ByDonkeys

It's not only Leavers who are marching.

A week from now there's going to be a huge rally, this time in London, this time Remainers, this time with more than seventy-seven people turning up. It's the big Put it to the People march, hundreds of thousands are expected and the organizers have asked us to be part of the moment. But we're fresh out of ideas. It's a great opportunity for a campaign group that's only been in existence for two months. We just can't think of anything to do.

'What about a building wrap?' says James towards the end of our third brainstorm. 'They can be massive. I once saw one down Oxford Street that covered a five-storey building. What about doing one of those on a building along the route?'

He calls up the organizers of the march, who are familiar with our campaign and seem to like what we do.

'Look, can you find us a building?' he asks.

'What kind of building do you want?'

'The biggest building you can find, I suppose. Something massive.'

To our surprise, the march organizers recruit a team of interns to go along the route, knocking on doors and going into shops and asking which random Russian oligarch owns this building, and can we ask for their permission to drop a massive anti-Brexit tweet banner off it? But we get nowhere.

We organize another Skype chat.

'What about those things they do in football stadiums?' says Ben. 'You know, where the crowd passes a massive

sheet over their heads. I mean *massive*. The size of the stadium. A huge tweet getting passed backwards along the route by hundreds of thousands of people. Could that work?'

'Oh, that could be good,' says Olly. 'But maybe in Parliament Square?'

'Imagine that Davis quote on it,' says James. 'The one about democracy. That would work.'

'If we can get the shot,' says Will, 'it would be immense.'

We use Google Maps to create a scaled mock-up of what this thing would look like from the air. It looks good. Really good. But by now it's the Monday before the march. Five days to go. How the hell are we going to make this happen?

James googles 'crowd flag' and calls the first company that comes up.

'What's the biggest flag you can give us?' he asks.

'Obviously this is very short notice,' says the woman at flags.co.uk.

'Five days?'

'It's tight.'

'But what can you get us?'

'For three thousand pounds we can get you a flag by Friday that's going to be fifteen metres by seven metres.'

'Okay, that sounds big. Thank you. But what is the absolute biggest you can give us? Something maybe – I don't know – forty metres by twenty metres?'

'That's going to be a lot of money.'

'What's a lot of money?'

'Twelve thousand, give or take.'

'But can you do it?'

'Yes. I mean, we'll have to ditch other work. Something this big, you have to print out the sections separately, then stitch them together. But yes, we can do it.'

'I'd like to order that one, please.'

Okay, we're committed now. But how do we get a picture of the thing being unfurled? It's illegal to operate drones next to Parliament, and the only buildings around there high enough to get the shot are the Palace of Westminster and Westminster Abbey. There's no way we'll be able to

get on those roofs. Will jumps on his laptop and googles 'London helicopter hire' and calls the first company that comes up. Ten minutes later he's spent another five grand. But we have a chopper for the big day.

Maybe it's poor project management, irresponsible accounting perhaps, but that's twice we've gone to the first company that popped up on Google and agreed to give them a huge sum of money to deliver an idea we've only just conceived. But that's how Led By Donkeys has rolled from the start. We don't have time for inquisitions and lengthy discussions; we're going on instinct, it's *deadlines deadlines deadlines*, but we're getting stuff done. Not long ago we were hoping for seven retweets off the Cameron poster, now we're hiring a helicopter. It's nuts, but we don't have time to dwell on it. There's too much work to do.

Back at the March to Leave, we've pulled one of our ad-vans and adopted a new rule: everything we post about the march must target Farage, not the marchers. We're getting messages from some of our followers saying the highlight of their day is checking the Led By Donkeys Twitter feed to get the latest risible attendance figures, but *where are the pictures of fat pink-faced ruddy wankers?* We have dozens of images that reinforce the stereotype of the splenetic Brexiter, but we're resisting the temptation to ridicule the protesters. At the end of leg four, when the marchers check into the Unicorn Hotel in Ripon, our resolve is severely tested.

Will: NOOO WAAYYYYYYY!!!! HA HA HA!!!!

Ben: Yes way. The Unicorn. Too good to not do it, right?

Olly: Actually guys we said we're not going to take the piss out of the marchers. Let's let it go

And we do. We've just hit 100k Twitter followers, in the process overtaking Michael Gove. We can let this one pass.

We've managed to maintain our anonymity for more than two months now, but our March to Leave operation has given the project a newly elevated profile. On social media, people are increasingly demanding to know who's behind it, and there are hostile attempts to log into our email and Twitter accounts. For the first time it seems everyone around us is following what we're doing; they just don't know it's us. James's partner spends the evening at the house of a family friend where the conversation is dominated by discussion of Led By Donkeys. She nods along, without revealing that she lives with one of them. At Greenpeace, Ben and Olly's colleagues cluster around a laptop to watch a video from the march, without knowing that half the Donkeys crew is sitting a few metres away.

By now our surplus ad-van is driving around London displaying a two-word message in huge letters: *Where's Nigel?* We know he's abandoned the march, he's not in a muddy field in Rutland, but where has he chosen to be instead? We park the van outside the East India Club in Mayfair, where he's a member, then send it to the Russian Embassy. The purpose is not simply to highlight Farage's absenteeism but, more importantly, to diminish him in the eyes of a news media with which he has an oddly symbiotic relationship. Too often they give him a platform in exchange for the drama he delivers. We want to change the story so that he's asked the hard questions about the numbers on his march and his abandonment of his followers.

We know our story is breaking through when former Belgian prime minister Guy Verhofstadt tweets:

> ⚪ I'm surprised to see you here [in Brussels], Mr Farage. I thought you were marching 200 miles for the leave campaign? How many did you do? 2 miles! You remind me more & more of Field Marshal Haig in Blackadder, sitting safely in his office, while his people are walking in the cold & the rain.

While it's gratifying to see our narrative resonating in Brussels, we know that's not where this battle will be won. But when Farage appears on Radio 4's *Today* programme and presenter Mishal Husain spends a good proportion of the conversation ribbing him for quitting after Hartlepool, we know our intervention has hit home. An irritated Farage sulks and scoffs his way through the interview, flinging familiar accusations of BBC bias, but his epic protest march has become little more than a punchline.

Job done.

We're hurtling towards the weekend and we don't know what we're doing. With no experience of deploying a crowd banner, let alone one this big, we're starting to worry. The eyes of the UK – perhaps of Europe – will be on Parliament Square on Saturday afternoon. But how will the banner unfurl? Will people help us or just stand and watch? What if there's panic underneath and we create a stampede? What if we lose control of the banner and it heads off down Whitehall and gets wrapped around the Cenotaph? Is it flammable? Could it immolate the People's Vote march and, with it, any hope of stopping Brexit?

All of this plays out on *#PosterChat* and over several sleepless nights. Olly (who is leading on logistics) wakes up suddenly with a cold start at 3 a.m., eyes wide open, having just pictured himself in Parliament Square with one hand through a corner strap on the banner, trying to walk through a dense crowd of confused Remainers who block his path. By Wednesday we're wobbling and close to calling it off, but we talk ourselves round, after Ben circulates a YouTube video of a huge crowd banner being deployed in a football stadium. It looks simple enough. *We can do this*, we think. *We're on.* We confirm with the march organizers and secure our slot on their stage.

Twenty-four hours to go. There's equipment to buy, a van to hire and pick up, volunteers to recruit. At 4 p.m. on Friday the banner is delivered to Olly's house. It's big. Really big. And heavy. It takes three of us to load it into the back of the van.

Saturday morning, 8 a.m., Finsbury Park. It's cloudy and cold but dry. Good news. The banner already comes in at 160kg, and a rain shower could double its weight. We're up early to take a first look at it unfolded and to work out how to deploy it. Friends and friends of friends have answered a late-night scramble on WhatsApp, and a handful of volunteers are in the park helping us figure out how this is going to work. James's friend Hannah has left her two kids at home with her partner, to be in the park, but she says she's not coming to Parliament Square.

'I can't deal with big crowds, and the thought of being under that thing fills me with dread,' she says.

Oh God. Really? What if some of the people in the square feel the same way, as the banner comes over their heads? The plan is to warn the crowd from the stage, so that nobody is involved involuntarily. But our anxiety rises another notch.

Six hours to go.

Meanwhile in the Nottinghamshire village of Linby, Nigel Farage has re-joined the March to Leave. Was it our *Where's Nigel?* van that forced him back? Maybe, maybe not. Either way, we're ready to target him again with his own words. We've cut a new video that we'll play on the giant mobile digital screen that we have following the march. While James and Olly concentrate on Parliament Square, Will and Ben are coordinating the March to Leave operation from Sweden and London. Will is hoping it runs smoothly, because he'll also be editing the crowd banner pictures and video and he'll be doing it all from an auditorium in Gothenburg, where he's taking his five-year-old son to see *PAW Patrol Live* – a show about a pack of hero search-and-rescue dogs that can turn into customized vehicles and are armed with powerful rucksacks called 'pup packs'.

It's been a week of tumultuous Brexit chaos in Parliament. There are just six days until Brexit Day, but the government can't get its deal passed. It looks like Theresa May is going to ask for a short extension to Article 50. What once seemed inevitable (the UK leaving the EU on 29 March) now looks unlikely. The forces of Remain have the

energy, but if we mess this up – if our banner is a shambles, if someone gets injured – then we'll be responsible for reversing that momentum and handing the advantage to the Leavers. On the other hand, the timing couldn't be better. Today hundreds of thousands of people will march on Parliament to demand that the Brexit decision is given back to the people. The quote on our 800 sq/m tweet is made for this moment.

The first video from Linby comes through. It shows Farage speaking from the open-top double-decker to a small crowd in a car park, but to the side of the bus our ad-van is playing footage of him campaigning in the recent Alabama Senate race for a man credibly accused of sexually assaulting children.*

Olly and James pull up at Parliament Square, get out of the van and stare at the space, then at each other, then back at the square. No words are needed. White-faced,

---

* The candidate denies the allegations and has not been charged in relation to the claims.

we're thinking the same thing. *Our banner won't fit.* The lawn is small and surrounded by white flagpoles that weren't visible on Google Earth. This isn't going to work. This is a disaster. It's over before we've even got the thing out of its bag. How could we have been so stupid? Why the hell didn't we come down to the square and measure it properly? But then James strides away, pacing the grass, and a minute later he's back.

'It's going to fit,' he says. 'Only just, but it fits.'

'Really?' says Olly.

'I think so. I mean I *hope* so.'

'You think we can risk it?'

'Yeah, I think we should.'

The square is still fairly empty. With a few hours to go before our scheduled time slot, we move the folded and packed banner out onto the grass alongside the stage. Now it's time to tell the organizers how it's all going to work. Olly and James head backstage to brief the rally coordinators, with whom we've been liaising over the banner plan.

It's a tiny space filled with well-known Remainers. Alastair Campbell steps forward and shakes James's hand.

'Love the Donkeys,' he says.

Next we're introduced to Steve Coogan, who's going to compère our slot from the stage. We explain what we're doing, and what we need him to tell the crowd to make the flag-unfurling work. He seems more nervous than we are.

Ben is also in the square with his one-year-old daughter on his shoulders. He's not part of the banner-deployment team because his partner will soon give birth and he needs to be able to leave at any moment. Around him he spots four or five people holding Donkeys tweets as placards. He's on his phone, sifting through the content coming in from the March to Leave and posting the best to social media. The latest video shows Farage leading the marchers down a country lane towards an ad-van playing footage of him getting busted by Channel 4 News for taking a private jet to work. When Farage sees the digital screen he veers away and leaves the road, trying to avoid being filmed in front of it. He skips along a verge, desperately trying to steer clear of our van, filmed all the way by our videographer. When Ben watches the video back he notices something. He watches it again to check. Can it be?

Ben: Oh my god when he swerves away watch the guy next to him. Nigel Farage in on this anti-elitist march and HE HAS A MANSERVANT TO CARRY HIS HAT AND COAT!

Will: RINSE!

Ben: Tweeting now

At Parliament Square the first marchers are arriving and the space is filling up fast. A bunch of our friends are here to help, while the crew from For our Future's Sake has recruited a team of volunteers as well. With an hour to go, everyone is assembled and on standby, and James is keeping in

touch with the helicopter team, who need a twenty-minute heads-up to take off and get into position above us.

One hundred and twenty miles away Nigel Farage has stopped for a pint in a beer garden. As he sips his ale and smokes a cigarette, surrounded by his followers,

an ad-van slowly reverses behind him, then stops. On the screen is footage of him on Channel 5's *The Wright Stuff* in 2018, and booming from the speakers is his voice declaring his support for a second referendum. He glances at the screen. The irritation on his face is obvious. His followers turn and watch the video. Farage exhales smoke and takes a swig of beer, but looks like he's swallowed a wasp. Our videographer captures the scene in all its excruciating beauty.

By 3.30 p.m. Parliament Square is packed. James calls the helicopter team and gives them the green light to go. They're on their way. Olly catches a glimpse of James, standing further along the length of the banner. Just time for a mutual slow shake of the head, as if to say, *Whose stupid idea was this?* But there's no going back now.

Steve Coogan comes onstage to big cheers. 'Who's heard of Led by Donkeys?' he asks.

A huge cheer goes up. We're used to online support, but these are real people's faces breaking into grins at the

mention of our project. Bizarre! The helicopter appears above our heads, Olly gives the signal to get ready to go and the message travels down the line of people standing along the length of the unfurled banner. Coogan introduces a video compilation of our billboards that Will cut yesterday. It plays out on the giant screen. We're seconds away now. The final frame closes. Our cue to start. Olly shouts out, 'Okay, let's go!' and we're away, heading out into the crowd while holding an unfurling 800 sq/m tweet above our heads and shouting, 'Coming through!'

It's working. People in the crowd know instinctively what to do. We're making good progress across the square now, the crowd reaching up to grab the banner and pull it forward. Instinctive cooperation. It's beautiful. And no sign of panic, just smiles and whoops. Soon we're close to the far side of the square. Will there be enough room? The flagpoles are getting closer. But just before we reach them, the banner pings taut. A big cheer goes up in the square and there are shouts and whistles down the line.

We did it! Hugs and high-fives are breaking out all around us. Amazing!

Ben looks up. There are two helicopters in the sky above him. He knows one of them is from the BBC and the other one is from Led By Donkeys. Just ten weeks ago he was covered in paste as he and Olly wrestled with a David Cameron poster off the A10. He squeezes his daughter's hand and mutters to himself, 'Well, this is fucking weird.'

Will is 650 miles away in Sweden in a huge out-of-town arena, amid thousands of kids cheering at their first sight of the *PAW Patrol* pups bursting onto the stage. The surrounding rows of parents glare scornfully as he pulls out his laptop, but the first pictures from the helicopter are dropping into WhatsApp and he needs to do an edit for the media. A familiar grating cartoon theme-song fills his ears as he scrolls through the images, but fades into the background as he focuses on the photos. Christ, they're spectacular. He picks out the best and shares them on *#PosterChat*. A minute later two video files drop. As he puts

on his headphones he can feel the disapproving eyes of other parents burning into him. He watches a film shot from the camera in the nose of the helicopter. Every last word of the banner is visible: a David Davis quote, rendered as a tweet across Parliament Square, that will soon spread around the world as the defining image of the march.

April 2019 ✔

@ByDonkeys

We're exhausted. Dog-tired and drained. We can't do this for much longer.

Ben's baby is due any day and he needs to step away from the project to be fully present at home. 'I love what you've done,' his partner Lorna tells him. 'I'm so proud of all of you. I just want to tell everyone that it's you. But I'm nearly nine months pregnant. I know Donkeys is your new baby, but I need our new baby to be your baby, if you know what I mean.' Ben does. Of course he does. He tells the others he'll do one more hit, then he's calling it quits.

Olly also needs to step away for a bit. The Easter holidays are approaching and the plan is to spend time together as a family: lots of fresh air, no phones. His partner, Emily, has been a huge support throughout – taking on extra school runs to facilitate late-night and early morning excursions. An experienced campaigner herself, she's also been a useful sounding board. But she and their daughters are in need of a few weeks where Brexit and Donkeys are dialled down.

Will is shattered and feels he's pushed his partner, Kajsa, to the limit. Before Parliament Square, he pulled a week of all-nighters to finish a redesign of Nigel Farage's BREAKING POINT poster, replacing asylum seekers with a swarm of Brexiters swamping Britain with their incompetence (we launched it on the exact same ad-van Farage used for the original – our small contribution to cleansing the nation of the stain left by that foul poster). Then came the March to Leave, helicopter hire and *PAW Patrol*. Now

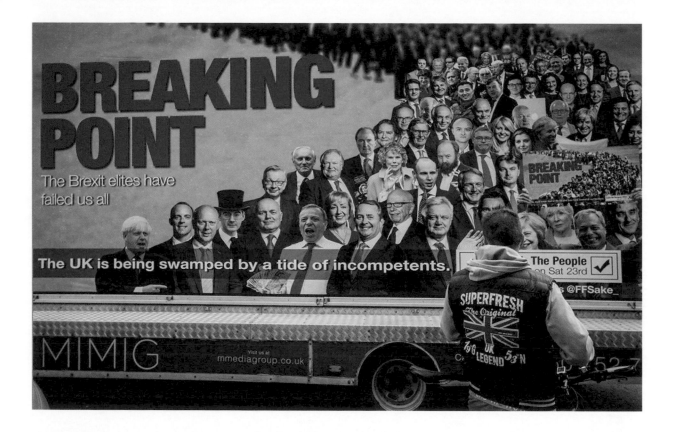

Will needs to spend quality time with his children, put his phone down and re-centre his life.

And James is the same. Although his partner, Tabs, wants him to push on (she wishes she'd gone up the ladder herself), he's burnt-out and feels like he hasn't seen enough of his kids.

We all want a break, but we can't kill Led By Donkeys. Not right now. Olly was in Parliament Square for the final leg of the March to Leave and saw far-right activist Tommy Robinson welcomed onto one of the two main stages by a crowd of several thousand people chanting his name. Olly can't walk away. None of us can.

By now Theresa May has been granted an extension to Article 50, so Brexit has been postponed by two weeks. The real prize is another, even longer delay that would give the forces of Remain the time to coalesce and persuade MPs to give the public a final say, but it's not clear if the EU will give Britain a long extension – it's said that Emmanuel Macron is ready to cut us loose, while Angela Merkel is more sympathetic. But Britain needs more time. The pro-Europe movement needs more time. Maybe we can send a message to Europe saying exactly that.

We chat to a friend of ours who projects messages onto buildings. He tells us he's just picked up some new kit, more powerful than anything he's used before. It projects as much light as a high-powered stadium floodlight, so should make for an incredible image. He needs to road-test it and wonders if we'd like to give it a spin. And yes, he'd be happy to trial it on the white cliffs of Dover.

Will starts working on a short film that we'll project across 3,000 sq/m of cliff face. We have an idea sparked by an incident on the March to Leave, where a woman in her seventies was standing on the route, clutching two little EU flags, as the Union Jack-waving march filed past, shouting abuse at her. *What a bad-ass*, we thought. But there was something about this clash of identities that bothered us. There's no need for those two flags to be in conflict. One of those twelve stars in the EU flag is ours – that's what

we think – and for as long as Britain remains a member of the EU, it will represent our country and its commitment to Europe.

We want to produce something that inspires the Remain movement, something that speaks to how far we've come in delaying Brexit and how far we can still go together. And we want to tell Brussels that we're not done yet, we just need more time.

Will's film tells the story of the six million people who've signed a petition demanding that Article 50 be revoked, before cutting to an SOS with the 'O' being the twelve yellow stars of the EU flag, and then to an image of a single yellow star on a blue background above the words: *THIS IS OUR STAR – WE'RE FIGHTING FOR IT*.

The projector is massive – way bigger than the ones you see in offices, this one is as big as an armchair. The team sets it up on a patch of ground in a wildlife reserve under the cliffs and, when the operator fires it up, the effect is stunning. The video is huge, the clarity remarkable. It's as if a flat-screen TV the size of a football pitch has been attached to the white cliffs of Dover.

First we project a tweet from our archive. It's one we've wanted to get up here since the moment the cliffs were first mooted as a potential canvas, something we'd never dreamt of doing when we first came to Dover three months ago with the ladder. Across the gigantic slab of cliff face we project Dominic Raab's fatuous imbecility: *I hadn't quite understood the full extent of this but... we are particularly reliant on the Dover–Calais crossing*. Then we play Will's video. It looks amazing. We'll later be messaged by a follower who tells us he saw it from the air as he was flying into Gatwick.

The next morning we post footage of the film playing on the cliffs. We accompany the video with a message to Europe in English, French and German:

Dominic Raab

I hadn't quite understood the full extent of this but... we are particularly reliant on the Dover-Calais crossing.

7 Nov 2018

He didn't tweet it, he actually **said** it! In a speech to the tech industry.

#LedByDonkeys @ByDonkeys

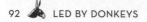

> Dear @EmmanuelMacron and Angela Merkel, opportunists from the hard right want Britain to crash out of Europe, even though a majority now wants to stay.
> We think the people should decide what happens next. But please give us more time.

The video is watched half a million times. Guy Verhofstadt, the former Belgian PM who is the EU Parliament's representative in the Brexit negotiations – one of the officials with the power to sway the decision on a long extension – tweets:

> Quite something to see the White Cliffs of Dover turn blue. But the European project is much more than a lifebuoy. It's our rock on which we have to build our future, especially in turbulent times.

Two days later Ben's partner has their baby, and a week after that Brexit is delayed until 31 October. It's time to shut down.

Olly, Will and James meet in a café to finalize the plan. It's going up tonight. Ben is on standby. Once we've got the poster up, he's going to jump in a car, join the others for the photo and then head home, aiming to be away from his partner and new baby for no more than half an hour. We're still anonymous, so we want to work quickly; put up the poster, take the photo and get home.

The last time we did this was three months ago and we're a little worried that we might have lost our guerrilla edge. And James is fretting about the message on the new poster we've had printed.

'I dunno,' he says. 'It kind of sounds a bit weak, don't you think? Like we're saying we failed. It sounds final – like we're giving up.'

Olly sucks his teeth. 'I know, I know. I've been thinking

the same. It makes it sound like we lost, but we didn't. We're still in Europe. Maybe we need to design a new one?'

'I have to go back to Sweden tomorrow,' says Will. 'And Ben's sorted it with Lorna that he can come out tonight. Guys, it has to be this evening.'

'Maybe we can edit this one?' says James. 'We've got two copies of it, right? A spare one in the car. If we cut up the letters on that one, we can make new words and change the message. You know, like kidnappers do with ransom notes, but for a massive billboard.'

'Do you think we could do that?' says Olly. 'Seriously?'

An hour later we're standing below the billboard site outside the Arsenal stadium. It's 10 p.m. Dark. We lay out the sheets on the pavement and start cutting out the letters. We're physically editing a billboard poster in the street and it's not discreet. Two guys stroll over and ask what we're doing. They look down at the pile of paper – segments of giant tweets – and ask if we've heard of Led By Donkeys, who they think are great. We tell them we're a sort of Donkeys tribute act. They wander away, unimpressed.

Once we've glued on the edits, we get the ladder up and start work. We're impatient to finish it – this is the first one we've done ourselves since the project really took off, and we're worried a passer-by might take a photo of us and share it on social media. But soon enough the four of us are standing together on the pavement in front of the billboard, our backs to the camera, arms draped over each other's shoulders, waiting for the timer to count down and take the photo we'll post across our social-media channels tomorrow morning.

Click!

We've pasted up Gove, Farage and Johnson. Now we've done a @ByDonkeys tweet.

> We started with a bucket of paste and a B&Q ladder. But thanks to you lot we managed to do so much more. We'll be back but we need to take a breather. Bye for now, LBD xx

May 2019 ✔

@ByDonkeys

Well, that didn't last long.

A fortnight after shutting it down, we're on a Skype call discussing the resurrection of the project. Farage is riding high in the polls, Theresa May is now in a semi-permanent state of imminent resignation (meaning a Tory leadership contest is coming and, with it, a No Deal political bidding war) and Donald Trump has confirmed he'll soon be visiting the UK on a state visit. It's a sordid trifecta of right-wing populist outrages and we're incapable of watching from the sidelines.

'We're not very good at taking a break, are we?' says Will.

'I dunno — we had a couple of weeks off,' says James. 'I'm feeling ready to get stuck back in.'

The idea is simple: Farage's newly formed Brexit Party has assembled a coterie of crackpots and extremists to run as candidates in the upcoming European elections, but they won't publish a manifesto. If the party won't tell us what their policies are, we're entitled to assume they're what the candidates have said are their core beliefs. So we'll run a short poster campaign informing the public of the positions that Farage and his crew have taken on the big issues.

We start digging into their pasts, throwing quotes into *#PosterChat*. Claire Fox was a member of the Revolutionary Communist Party (RCP) — a now-disbanded sect that went so far left it came out the other side — and now she's running for the Brexit Party in the north-west

region. In 1993 the RCP defended the IRA's murder of two children in Warrington, and the father of one of the boys is asking voters to reject Fox. Another candidate, James Bartholomew (south-east region), has said 'the people are generally wrong and stupid' and, like Farage, he's called for the privatization of the NHS.

We start turning the statements into tweet posters (that's what we're known for, right?), but quickly think better of it. Tweets don't work here. We need to explain that these quotes are our best guess at the policy platform of the Brexit Party and that requires a different approach. So Will starts working on mock-manifesto posters, while James turns thebrexitparty.com (which we registered a few weeks ago) into a repository for our Farage manifesto.

Because Electoral Commission rules state that anyone spending more than £20k on election campaigning must register their names, we limit the scope of the push. The attacks on the likes of Gina Miller and other high-profile Remainers have been vicious, and we're keen to avoid the tsunami of abuse that we assume would come our way if our names were made public. So we cap our outlay at £18k and check in with the Electoral Commission and a specialist lawyer to ensure we're not breaking any rules.

Exactly one month after putting up the @ByDonkeys poster opposite the Arsenal stadium, we go live with the new campaign. Our opening salvo is a familiar Farage quote (*We need to move to an insurance-based system of healthcare*) on a poster in Coventry.

The reaction is gratifying. It seems people have been craving a campaign that takes on the new party. Soon enough the poster has been seen two million times on social media, mainstream news outlets are bombarding us with calls and the whole thing is taking off. Next up is Bartholomew on the NHS, then Farage's attack on a European Parliament vote extending maternity pay. The plaudits are flowing. We congratulate ourselves on having produced a brilliant intervention in the European elections.

They say pride comes before a fall. For us, it is

accompanied by a dose of arrogance and a failure of judgement.

The following day is a Friday. We have pictures of six more newly pasted posters to tweet out, but we decide the next one will be Brexit Party candidate Ann Widdecombe declaring, 'Homosexual acts are wrongful.' Soon enough the picture of the poster in the Dorset town of Christchurch races past 3,000, 4,000, 5,000 retweets. Another successful deployment. We're on a roll here. Then around lunchtime James is scrolling through our Twitter mentions when he sees a response by *Guardian* columnist Owen Jones. James's stomach turns. He feels physically sick. Owen deletes the tweet a minute later, but it's immediately clear to James that we've messed up.

James calls *#PosterChat*. The others know something has happened because the WhatsApp group is usually used only for texting. Calls are reserved for emergencies.

'Guys, did you see what Owen Jones tweeted?'

'Nope.'

'No.'

'Something bad?'

'He's deleted it now, but he said he hopes people in Christchurch tear down the Widdecombe poster. He says it's offensive to put up homophobic quotes on a billboard – people won't get that it's against Farage, and they'll think it's just an anti-gay campaign.'

'What are other people saying?'

'Hang on,' says James. He puts himself on speakerphone and scrolls through the mentions. 'Yeah, okay, there's a few of them coming through now. They're basically saying this is hate-speech put on a massive billboard in a town centre. And Owen's retweeted someone else. It says, *As a gay man I really, really don't think plastering billboards with "Homosexual acts are wrongful" is going to be as subversive or progressive as you seem to think.*'

'I mean, he's right,' says Olly.

'He just is,' says Ben.

'God, he is,' says Will.

'We have to take it down,' says James. 'We have to get it taken down and delete the tweet and apologize.'

For all of us it is quite comfortably the worst moment of the campaign. We've caused pain to the very group of people we wanted to stand in solidarity with, and it's entirely our fault. Within a few minutes James has booked a billboard-paster to cover up the poster that afternoon. In *#PosterChat* we work on the wording of an apology, and twenty minutes later we've posted it.

> We've been getting some justified criticism today on social media for posting a billboard of Ann Widdecombe's homophobic views. So we're taking the billboard down and deleting the tweet. Just because we're outraged by her views, it doesn't mean everyone will be, and more importantly there will be some who take her words at face value. If it's causing pain and anger to those directly affected by

> homophobia it's totally counterproductive. Really sorry everyone, we fucked that one up. Love LBD xx

All of us feel sick with shame for having upset people in the gay community. Maybe this is the end of the project? Christ, maybe it should be. We're four straight guys who didn't take a moment to consider how other people would experience the poster. Heady with our success, we just ploughed ahead, unthinking. We're idiots and we deserve everything that's coming our way.

As it is, the comments beneath the apology are forgiving. Some even berate us for taking the poster down. But we know we've made a big mistake. Ben feels like he needs some air and tells his partner he's going to take his older daughter to the shops to exchange a jumper she got as a present. A few minutes later he's on a bus, one hand on the handle of the pushchair and the other scrolling through reactions to the apology, when he

sees a tweet from Guido Fawkes, the hard-right website that trades in smears and personal destruction and has close links to the Brexit Party.

> ⬤ @GuidoFawkes – EXC: Anti-Brexit Billboard Campaign 'Led By Donkeys' in Massive Apparent Breach of Electoral Law

Excuse me – what?!

The tweet links to an article claiming we've spent more – much more – than the £20k limit and therefore should have registered with the Electoral Commission. They calculated we've put up hundreds of billboards at an estimated cost of £1,000 each, so not only have we crashed through the £20k threshold, they say we've also passed the absolute limit of spending £160k in the run-up to an election.

It's nonsense. The vast majority of our spending had absolutely nothing to do with the Euro elections; it went on billboards that were put up while the government was insisting there wouldn't even be elections to the EU Parliament. We know, from talking to the Electoral Commission, that they have no intention of counting a John Redwood poster from January towards our electioneering spend. Ben reverses the pushchair off the bus and directs it through the department store doors and into the children's clothes section. He puts on his headphones and calls *#PosterChat*.

'Have you seen this Guido thing?' he says.

'Just read it,' says Olly. 'It doesn't rain, it pours.'

'It's crap,' says James. 'Shows we're pissing them off.'

'They're just the Brexit Party press shop, right?' says Will.

'Yeah, but they know what they're doing,' says Ben, pushing his daughter past a rack of pyjamas, looking for a jumper in the toddler-size range. 'The Brexit Party's getting all this heat from the media saying their funding looks a bit dodgy, so now Guido's trying to set us up as the real dark-money villains. *Who's behind this shadowy anonymous Remain outfit that's raised all this money but*

won't register with the Electoral Commission? Seriously, guys, we're being set up.'

'God, you're right,' says Olly. 'This is about diverting attention from Farage. They want to change the story to make it about us. If we don't kill it, the danger is it rolls on and gets bigger.'

'Exactly,' says Ben. 'They'll hammer us till we're the story.'

'So what do we do?' says Will.

'I think we need to come out and say who we are,' says Ben.

Silence.

'Seriously?' says James.

'Big call,' says Will.

'I think you might be right,' says Olly.

'It's Friday afternoon,' says Ben. 'Nothing's going to happen between now and Monday, but we need to make a call after the weekend. Have a think about it. Obviously it would be a big deal. Anyway, guys, I have to go, I'm in Marks & Spencer.'

'Okay, bye.'

'Bye.'

'Let's check in later.'

Each of us has a restless weekend. The Widdecombe poster has knocked our confidence, while the funding story has put us on notice that anonymity has run its course. We stay off Twitter and tell each other to put Donkeys to the back of our minds and instead give time and energy to our families. But it's hard. After four months of running the table, with everything we put out seemingly pushing the needle for Remain, raising hundreds of thousands of pounds and building a Twitter following of 200k people, suddenly the four of us are weighed down with imposter syndrome. *We're out of our depth here. We pissed off Farage on the March to Leave and now his people are coming after us. We got too big for our boots. The Widdecombe poster and Guido Fawkes in the space of two hours. Maybe it's time to just pack it all in?*

We take our kids to the park, soft-play, out to the woods

— all of us trying to stay off our phones. But we're all mulling over the next step. And by Monday, when we meet on a Skype call, we're agreed on what to do next.

We're deflated. And we're a bit scared. We know we have to come out and say who we are, but the prospect of receiving abuse and threats is frightening. The comments beneath articles on the Guido blog are often peppered with disgusting, hateful language, and we've been told a Tommy Robinson supporter is trying hard to find out who we are. Nevertheless we take the plunge and register with the Electoral Commission, giving our full names. We haven't spent more than the £20k threshold on the Euro elections, but we think it's the right thing to do.* We won't let the Brexit Party paint us as a secret outfit operating in the shadows. It's time to live our values.

We assume it will take a few days for our names to be published online. Ben calls the *Observer* and offers the newspaper the exclusive — an interview that reveals who we are. We arrange to meet their reporter in The Birdcage on Wednesday, two days from now. The morning of the interview James pings a screenshot from the Electoral Commission website to *#PosterChat*, then calls the group.

'Argh, sorry, guys,' he says. 'Our names are up. Happened already.'

'Here we go then,' says Olly.

'It is what it is,' says Will. 'I guess we'll get turned over now.'

'Maybe they won't spot it,' says James. 'It'd be good to have the *Observer* thing out first.'

'Not gonna happen,' says Ben. 'I reckon we've got a few hours at most. I'm gonna take my Twitter and Facebook down. Don't want weirdo journos scrolling down pictures of me with my kids.'

'Yeah, me too,' says Will.

'Same,' says James.

---

* The Electoral Commission will later write to us confirming that we broke no spending rules.

That afternoon we sit with the *Observer* journalist at the same table where a few months earlier we decided to put up Cameron's tweet on a billboard across the road. As expected, the Guido Fawkes site has published a new attack in the form of a video, again focusing on our anonymity and the nonsense claim that we've spent more than the legal limit. But nothing yet on our identities.

'Okay,' says Harriet from the *Observer*. 'Let's start off by asking who you actually are.'

We go round the table.

'Ben Stewart.'

'James Sadri.'

'Oliver Knowles.'

'Will Rose.'

She scribbles down our names. No going back now. We speak for an hour, telling her about that first night across the road from here when we wrestled with Cameron, in a shower of undercooked wallpaper paste; how we never really wanted to go legit; how we pulled off the March to Leave and Parliament Square; and why we think it's time now to show our faces.

The *Observer*'s photographer lines us up and takes our picture, then he and Harriet leave. We sit alone at the table, sipping our pints and deconstructing the interview. We're pretty sure we gave a good account of ourselves. The question now is whether it comes out before we're turned over by the Brexit Party. Then Will's phone pings. He looks down and grimaces.

'A text from a mate,' he says. 'We've been Guido-ed.'

We cluster over the screen: *EXCLUSIVE: Led By Donkeys unmasked as Greenpeace campaigners*.

There's a photograph of each of us, above a short article detailing our activist history and some biographical details lifted from the Internet.

'It says I'm Director of Special Projects at Greenpeace,' says Ben. 'I haven't done that job for years. Where did they get that from?'

'LinkedIn, I think,' says Will.

'I didn't even know I have a LinkedIn account. Is that why they keep sending me alerts saying people want to connect with me?'

'This actually isn't too bad,' says James. 'I mean they say we all work for Greenpeace and I haven't done anything for Greenpeace for six years, but since when was working for Greenpeace a scandal?'

'Yeah, I've only ever done freelance work for GP,' says Will. 'So they got that wrong.'

'God, I don't even remember setting it up,' says Ben. 'I hate LinkedIn.'

'Is this all they've got?' asks Olly. 'Seems a bit of a non-event. Stop press: some campaigners are campaigning. I expected something about what Ben did when he was fourteen.'

'The question is whether the pro-Brexit papers do something before the *Observer*,' says James.

'I want to know what Ben did when he was fourteen,' says Will.

We all feel something close to relief. The anticipation of being unmasked was, so far at least, worse than the reality. But we're still wary. Our names are out there and we've had enough crazy messages on Twitter over the past four months to know this could still get nasty.

It's nearly 5 p.m., time to pick up kids from after-school clubs and nursery. We embrace and go our separate ways, telling each other to check in if we start getting threats, but as it happens, the evening passes off without drama. We get a couple of messages from friends – *You're Led By Donkeys?! Why didn't you tell me? I've followed you from the start!* – but it seems Guido's revelation hasn't registered out there. The Guido blog has declined in influence in recent years and now we're wondering if we've been savaged by a paper tiger. We've taken down our social-media accounts, meaning we haven't had any personal abuse (though the Greenpeace office is being targeted by trolls). And by the time we've put the kids to bed and checked in on *#PosterChat* we're feeling relatively sanguine.

Over Thursday and Friday we keep an eye on the press. Nothing. *The Times* puts in a request for the first interview, but we've already spoken to a rival paper. The big question now is whether the *Observer* interview will be negative, perhaps focusing on the Widdecombe poster and Guido's baseless smears, or something more complimentary. It feels like the future of the project depends on how we're depicted in the article.

On Saturday morning we're out with our kids. Olly is on the first day of a family holiday in the Lake District, James is bringing his daughter back from gym class, Will is at home playing Lego with his eldest, and Ben is at a soft-play centre.

A friend messages him saying that she's just read the profile on the *Guardian* website and *Holy shit, I never knew you were the one behind those posters*. Quickly Ben extracts his daughter from a bouncy castle, puts her on his knee and, with a pounding heart, skim-reads the interview. Then he takes to *#PosterChat*.

Ben: It's up and it's brilliant

Five minutes later...

James: Big phew!

Will: It's amazing. Makes you feel pretty good about doing all this

Olly: So much love in the mentions. Thank god it's a lovely piece

We put our private social-media accounts back up. The trolls find us soon enough, but the abuse is tolerable. A red-faced man in an ill-fitting, bright-blue pinstripe suit calls Olly a parasite, but that's about as bad as it gets. By the end of the weekend we're sure there's life left in Led By Donkeys, which is a relief, because eight days from now our country will be graced by a state visit from Donald Trump.

Trump and Brexit are two sides of the same coin. The US president has used his megaphone to agitate for No Deal, and has been adulatory about Farage and current Tory leadership front-runner Boris Johnson. He'll clearly use his platform in London to try and influence the Brexit debate. Moreover, Trump will use images of himself amidst the ceremonial splendour of a state visit to burnish his credentials back home, no doubt claiming the British people and their Royal Family embraced him with tremendous enthusiasm.

Our objectives are to diminish Farage through his association with the unpopular president; embarrass Johnson before a mooted meeting with Trump; and let the American people know that their president is radioactively unpopular here. We book two double billboard sites and recruit the projector team. The plan is to project the *Access Hollywood* tape ('Grab 'em by the pussy...') onto Buckingham Palace during the president's state dinner, and to paste up the most explosive section of the tape onto half the giant billboards, with Farage and Johnson's fawning adulation for Trump on the other half. But we're having second thoughts. The Widdecombe episode has taught us an important lesson. We're four men who lead similar lives, and not everyone experiences our interventions the same way we do – and that definitely goes for more sensitive material like the *Access Hollywood* tape. So we ask our partners what they make of our plans.

'On Buckingham Palace?' says Olly's partner, Emily.

'Yup.'

'During the big state dinner.'

'That... that is the working plan, yes.'

'You're going to project a man talking about grabbing a woman's vagina onto a ninety-three-year-old woman's house while she's hosting a dinner party? You don't think having to host Trump is bad enough for her?'

'It's just an idea.'

It's no longer an idea. We develop new concepts for the projections and drop the 'p' word from the billboards. Footage exists from three years ago of Johnson talking about Trump in the most excoriating language. It would be a major embarrassment to both men if it got a high-profile airing on the eve of their meeting. Okay, we'll project that instead. But where? It has to be somewhere instantly recognizable to an American audience. The projector team starts searching through London guidebooks and cross-referencing potential locations with Google Street View to see what might work.

The recent renovation of Elizabeth Tower (what everyone calls Big Ben) has seen a giant white scaffold cover stretched across the bottom quarter. It's like a cinema screen. Perfect for what we have planned. And the Tower of London looks suitable for an image of Trump's woeful UK approval rating (21 per cent) set against Obama's (72 per cent). And onto the Planetarium dome of Madame Tussauds we'll project a picture of a USS *John S. McCain* baseball cap. Why? Because *The Wall Street Journal* has just reported that on Trump's recent trip to Japan his White House ordered that the ship have its name covered in tarpaulin, because the vessel is named after the deceased US Senator who blocked Trump's abolition of Obamacare, and whom Trump despises. The ship's crew was also given the day off so that Trump wouldn't have to see the name on their baseball caps. So we'll make sure he sees it here.

With Trump in the air over the Atlantic, the projector team deploys.

First up is Big Ben. Boris Johnson across 200 sq/m of the globally iconic monument, his words coming out of a speaker the size of a suitcase. People stop to film it on their phones. 'I think Donald Trump is clearly out of his mind,' Johnson booms. 'What he is doing is playing the

 Led By Donkeys
@ByDonkeys

Hey @realDonaldTrump, you just endorsed your Brexit buddy @BorisJohnson but he said some VERY NASTY things about you and he doesn't want you to know. So we projected his words onto Big Ben. Watch with the SOUND ON #TrumpUKVisit

game of the terrorists... When Donald Trump says there are parts of London that are no-go areas I think he is betraying a quite stupefying ignorance that makes him frankly unfit to hold the office of President of the United States. I would invite him to come and see the whole of London and take him round the city, except I wouldn't want to expose Londoners to any unnecessary risk of meeting Donald Trump.'

You can see by their expressions that the spectators get what we're doing here. They're laughing and nodding, and even doing that most un-London of things and talking to strangers about the projection. We run through the video six or seven times, filming it from different angles, capturing the public's reaction. But then a couple of cops come round the corner and approach our team. Johnson's face is quickly pulled from Big Ben and replaced with a huge message in metre-high letters that tower over the officers' heads: **SUPPORT YOUR LOCAL POLICE FORCE**. The cops glance up. A smile touches the corners of their lips, but they're not fooled.

'Time to move along.'

'Righto.'

It's fine – we have what we need. Next stop is the Tower of London and Trump's UK approval rating, then sometime after 1 a.m. the team is on the pavement opposite Madame Tussauds, projecting the *McCain* hat onto the dome.

Six hours later the Big Ben video has been edited and we have stunning photos from the other sites. Trump is about to land. We publish Johnson at 8 a.m. It's the first time we've posted an intervention since our names were revealed and we wonder if the reaction will be muted. Has the project lost its appeal since we outed ourselves and gave up the mystery that comes with anonymity? But within minutes the video has raced away to 10,000, 20,000, 50,000 views. (It will eventually be watched two million times, and Johnson's meeting with Trump will be cancelled.)

We post the Tower of London photo at lunchtime (morning rush hour on the US east coast), then the McCain hat at mid-afternoon UK time. We hadn't expected this to

be a particularly big day for us, but the images in those three tweets end up being viewed more times than anything we've done so far, including Parliament Square. Between them, they're seen twelve million times on people's Twitter feeds. The projections appear across the nightly news broadcasts on the big US television networks; Stephen Colbert includes the Tower of London photo in his iconic opening monologue on *The Late Show*; on MSNBC Rachel Maddow runs a three-minute report on the Johnson video; the crowd on *The Daily Show* cheers when the Tower of

London picture is shown; *USA Today* runs the headline **USS John S. McCain hats sell out online after London protest**; and on ABC's *The View* Whoopi Goldberg and McCain's daughter Meghan revel in the Madame Tussauds photo.

'It made me and my mother laugh so hard,' Meghan McCain says. 'The way that British people troll, they do it so much better than we do.'

James: Trump's on Twitter slagging off the Maddow report

Olly: Ha! Means he's seen the Big Ben video

Will: Definitely seen it

Ben: 👊 💥 🐴

Epilogue ✔
@ByDonkeys

In a post-industrial wasteland beneath a Led By Donkeys billboard Boris Johnson is trying to resuscitate a dead badger with a cattle-prod. Nigel Farage looks on from a discarded mattress, as Michael Gove jogs past an 8ft tall Slovakian demon-chaser. On the billboard are Johnson's words from his time as foreign secretary: *There is no plan for no deal because we're going to get a great deal.*

The tableau is a collaboration between us and the artist Cold War Steve, whose previous commission was to design the cover of *Time* magazine. The work has been printed out on a 6 x 3m sheet and is debuting on a billboard at the Glastonbury Festival.

The four of us are here for our first night out together since that evening six months ago when we passed round a phone displaying Cameron's tweet. Since then we've raised more than £400,000, put up 300 anti-Brexit billboards, persuaded a quarter of a million people to follow us on Twitter and produced more than fifty poster designs that have been seen 200 million times online. We've sparked conversations in villages, towns and city centres across the country and have made famous the lies and hypocrisy of the leading Brexiters. Thousands of people have drawn strength from the campaign, and a fair few have hated it. Some Leavers have been converted, though most haven't budged. We sank Nigel Farage's March to Leave by administering a comprehensive rinsing – but two months later his new party topped the poll in the European elections. We haven't stopped Brexit, but

Glastonbury 2019 (Photograph: Cold War Steve/Led By Donkeys)

maybe we've made it just a little less likely.

Alastair Campbell thinks so. After Parliament Square, he tweeted:

> When the special 'they stopped Brexit' honours list is announced (a few years after the public inquiry) a special award like those sometimes given to special forces will be given to the secret heroes of @ByDonkeys.

And radio presenter James O'Brien tweets:

> For me, the single biggest journalistic failure of the last three years has been the refusal to remind politicians of their own words. It's such a simple thing to do and seems so important. @ByDonkeys, who are neither journalists nor politicians, have put us all to shame.

In *Campaign* magazine – the trade journal for the advertising industry – the chairman of Saatchi & Saatchi writes: *It's only halfway through 2019 but an early contender for agency of the year is surely Led by Donkeys... Its work is powerful, its growth prodigious and its impact historic... Led by Donkeys has proved there is life yet in posters, once the medium of choice for political campaigning.*

Crikey. The praise – albeit some of it from an industry we're innately suspicious of – is a welcome buttress for our sometimes-fragile confidence and encourages us to keep the project going.

It's now the end of June and Britain is an observer in the contest to choose the next prime minister, with Boris Johnson facing off against Jeremy Hunt. The result will define the minority government's approach to Brexit as the EU's Halloween deadline approaches, but 99.7 per cent of us have precisely no say whatsoever in the outcome. It seems clear to us that the Tory membership – older, whiter, more male and more wedded to No Deal than the country

it governs – will choose Johnson, so we've just launched a new crowdfunded ad campaign calling out his assorted violations against truth and consistency.

In some senses this is a dispiriting time to be a Remainer in Brexit Britain. The new vehicle for Farage's ego has twenty-nine MEPs, despite fielding a slate of crackpots whose views would, in saner times, be disqualifying. And the hardest of hard Brexits – No Deal – has become the hill on which the Leave elite is now prepared to die, notwithstanding previous assertions that abandoning the Single Market would be the act of a madman.

It feels like our country – this place that we're just as proud as they are to call home – has gone a little bit bonkers.

But there's nothing quite like standing in a sun-drenched field with a quarter of a million ecstatic souls to restore your faith in Britain. We're not so naive as to think Glastonbury is somehow representative of the nation as a whole, but this place does feel very far indeed from the world of splenetic ERG oddballs obsessing about a war that was fought and won by other people before they were born. This festival is the very antithesis of a Brexit Party rally. People talk openly of love and solidarity. There is a discernible absence of fear. And the music's better.

If a country is its culture, then there's hope for ours. Where else would a probation officer who makes surreal dystopian collages on his phone featuring demon-chasers become the unofficial artist-in-residence of the greatest political shitshow in living memory? In which other country, in the middle of the afternoon, would you pass a woman on stilts being followed like ducklings by her two kids (also on stilts) as the Love Unlimited Synth Orchestra plays on a stage behind. Is there another gathering on Earth where the world's most famous performers are upstaged by a ninety-three-year old presenter of natural history programmes, who speaks from the main stage to rapturous applause about the need to combat plastic pollution? And where else would this festival be televised across all

channels on the state broadcaster, so that every year it becomes a national moment?

A Britain that hosts the best and biggest party on the planet is one that can still find its way back home.

In common with everyone else, we can't be sure what will happen next. Maybe the charlatan who's about to become prime minister will succeed in pulling us out of the EU on Halloween. But at least we won't just be sitting on the sofa shouting at the news. There are too many new examples of sophistry and hypocrisy to get up on billboards, not least by Johnson himself. And Nigel Farage and his band of populist kooks are going nowhere. By the time we arrive at Glastonbury we've decided to throw everything we have at Led By Donkeys and the campaign, win or lose.

In a rented garage round the corner from his house, James is storing a new crowd banner. We're not sure where we'll unfurl this one, but there's going to be another march in London soon. No sleepless nights this time; we know what we're doing now. It's big. Bigger even than the banner we deployed in Parliament Square. On it is a huge yellow star on a blue background and a simple slogan in 2m high letters.

'This is our star. We're fighting for it.'

How to put up a billboard poster in eight steps

1 DESIGN

Your billboard is printed on twelve sheets. When designing your poster, as far as possible avoid placing words on the lines that divide those sheets — that way you'll make it easier to align the words when you deploy. Size and scale specifications for 6 x 3m billboards are available online.

2 DELIVERY DAY

Unpack the twelve sheets and lay them flat on the floor. They overlap by 2cm when they go up, so mark up two lines in the corner of each sheet — one 2cm in from the horizontal edge and another 2cm in from the vertical edge. Again, this makes it easier to align the sheets when you paste them.

3 PACKING

Roll them from the bottom up, so that when you're in action they unroll from the top down. Fasten them with masking tape and write the number of the sheet on the roll (sheets 1–6 are the top row, sheets 7–12 are the bottom row).

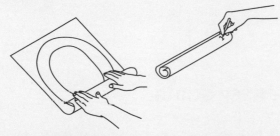

PRO TIP: One way to minimize blisters and bubbles is to briefly immerse your rolled sheets in a cold bath for about thirty seconds. Then pack the 12 rolls in a bin bag.

4 TO THE STREETS

It's time. You will need: two buckets of thick paste; one soft-bristle brush; one small hand-held pasting brush or roller; one 5m ladder; a determination to own the space.

5 IT BEGINS

Paste over the top-left sheet of the billboard you're replacing. Unpick the masking tape on sheet 1 and roll it down over the pasted area, brushing over the sheet as you go (with your smaller pasting brush or roller) and keeping it lined up exactly with the one you're covering up. Leave the bottom 5cm of your new sheet unpasted.

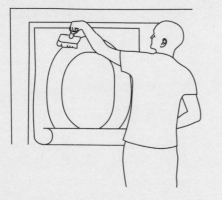

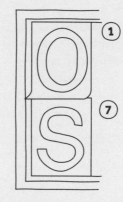

6 KEEP GOING

Paste sheet 7 below sheet 1. Use the horizontal lines you drew back at HQ to ensure there is a 2cm crossover between the sheets, with the top of sheet 7 tucked under the bottom of sheet 1. Now brush down the bottom of sheet 1 (that 5cm you left unpasted).

7 YOU'RE ON A ROLL NOW

Sheet 2 is next. Again, the trick here is to use your 2cm lines (this time the vertical ones) to make sure it's correctly aligned with sheet 1. The left side of sheet 2 goes over the right side of sheet 1. After that comes sheet 8 below it. Then repeat across the board — sheets 3 and 9, then sheets 4 and 10, etc.

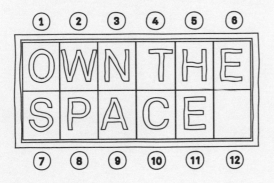

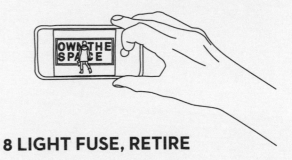

8 LIGHT FUSE, RETIRE

Stand back. Admire your work. Photograph it. Post to social media. Await results.

Acknowledgements

So many people have helped us out along the way, but we'd like to say a special thank you to:

Alex Rose, Alice Ross, Alice Russel, Amanda Chetwynd-Cowieson, Anna Llewellyn, Anna Nolan, Aram Martirossian, Blondie, Carl Gosling, Charlie Pounds, Chris Ratcliffe, Chris Spencer, Colin Rose, Courteny Andrews, Dafydd Trystan, Dan Flavell, Dan Gorman, Dan Green, Daniel Stent, Daphne Christelis, Dean Atkins, Doug Jackson, Elahe Pope, Eleanor Smith, Elika Aspinall, Eliza Guerrini, Emily Eavis, Farrah Jarral, Femi Oluwole, Fionn Guilfoyle, Fred Rood, Gavin Millar, Geraint Talfan Davies, Graeme Furley, Graeme Robertson, Graham Thompson, Guy Guerrini, Hagop Tchaparian, Hannah Richards, Harry Newington, Ian Bohn, Irene Rose, Jack Finn Taylor, James Hansen, Jan Stewart, Janire Najera, Jason Arthur, Jeremy Sutton-Hibbert, Jiri Rezac, John McConnico, John Wood, Jon Super, Josie Naughton, Kristian Buus, Linda Maitland, Luke MacGregor, Marie Stewart, Mark Harvey, Mark Hooper, Mark Stewart, Martin Pope, Matt Knifton, Matt Wright, Maureen Dealey, May Abdalla, Mishelle Stewart, Murry Toms, Nick Dewey, Nigel Roddis, Olivier Bonavero, Onur Uyar, Paul Box, Paul Finn, Paul Sherlock, Pete Christelis, Pete Vilk, Peter Gilbey, Phil Bonavero, Rachel Murray, Rachel Quick, Richard Brooks, Richard Stewart, Robin Turner, Roxana Vilk, Russell Todd, Said Durra, Sam Keyte, Sam Knowles, Simon Deverell, Steve Morgan, Steve Wilkinson, Suzanne Ireland, Suzanne Plunkett, Tim Dirven, Tim Dixon, Tricia Stewart and Yasmin Fedda.

THIS IS OUR STAR
WE'RE FIGHTING FOR IT